JOHN WESLEY
POWELL

Canyon's Conqueror

John Wesley Powell:

ILLUSTRATED BY HARVE STEIN

Canyon's Conqueror

MARIAN T. PLACE

HOUGHTON MIFFLIN COMPANY · BOSTON

NEW YORK · ATLANTA · GENEVA, ILL. · DALLAS · PALO ALTO

Contents

CHAPTER 1

A Real School

Nine-year-old Wes Powell wakened very early one September morning in 1843. A woodpecker was hammering loudly on the roof a few feet above his head.

"Go away," he said sleepily. He covered his head with the blanket to shut out the noise. His bed was on the second floor of a yellow frame house in the small settlement of Jackson, in southern Ohio.

Wes liked to waken to the music of bird song. Many robins and bluebirds nested in the oak trees nearby. But it was too early for them to start their sunrise chatter. Even the roosters in the barnyard behind the house were still silent.

"Rat-a-tat-a-tat!" the woodpecker pounded again, and again.

Wes stuck his fingers in his ears, but it was no use. He could still hear the sharp pecking. He reached under the bed for a shoe and tossed it against the roof.

"Chur-chur!" the woodpecker cried out, and flew away.

Plunk! The shoe dropped back onto Wes's pillow.

For a second he was too surprised to move. He rubbed the sleep from his gray eyes and pushed his dark, reddish-brown hair back from his forehead. Then he looked out the window.

Fog blanketed everything. Raindrops ran down the glass pane.

"Rain, rain, go away!" he chanted. He wasn't the least bit afraid of fog, like his two older sisters, Martha and Mary. They never went out when it was foggy. Some time ago they had tried to tell Wes that spooks hid in the fog.

"Aw, you can't scare me!" Wes had answered.

Today he remembered his sisters' attempt

to frighten him and wondered about it. Hurriedly he pulled on his clothes and ran downstairs. After swallowing a few spoonfuls of hot oatmeal, Wes asked his mother, "There aren't spooks hiding in the fog, are there?"

"Gracious, no!" his mother answered.

"What is fog, anyway?"

Mrs. Powell was rolling out pie crust. "Not another question! If your sisters asked as many questions as you do, I'd never finish my baking." But she was smiling. She knew Wes never asked silly questions to bother her. "Well, fog is made up of very tiny drops of water floating in the air."

"The same as a cloud?" Wes asked, a little puzzled.

"I think the difference between fog and a cloud is that fog is always near the ground." She lifted the dough into a pie pan and filled it with sliced peaches. "I wish I knew more about it. I never had nature studies when I went to school. It's too bad we don't have a dictionary. Then we'd both know for sure."

Before her marriage in London, England,

fifteen years earlier, Wes's mother had planned to be a teacher. Instead, she married tall and good-looking Joseph Powell, a Methodist minister. Soon after that, Reverend Powell came to America to carry the word of God to far-off settlements. First he held church services in western New York State. Later he moved with his growing family to southern Ohio.

At first the family did not live close to a real school. Mrs. Powell taught her children their letters and to read the Bible. She began with Martha and Mary, the two older girls. For an hour or two each day she held "school" at the kitchen table. After Wes was born, she held him on her lap during "school." By the time he was four, he knew his a-b-c's. Now he studied the same spelling and arithmetic as fourteen-year-old Martha and thirteen-year-old Mary.

"Tell me some more about fog," Wes begged. He was always wanting to know more about nature.

Mrs. Powell rolled the top crust for the

pie before answering. "No more questions, young man. Find out for yourself what fog is like when you go outside. It's time you cleaned the barn."

Wes liked to think for himself. So, on the way to the barn, he paid extra attention to the fog. He discovered that fog was a chilly wetness. It was thick, yet he could not grasp it. It did not come down in drops like the rain. It made the ground so slippery that he slid on his bare heels. Ugh! It made the pump handle slimy. He turned his face to the sky. He even tried to taste it.

While he cleaned the barn, his mind worked faster than his hands. "I wish we had a dictionary," he thought. Then he would not have to ask so many questions. He could discover for himself what words meant. That was more fun than being told everything. He always had liked hunting for rocks, for birds' nests, and insects, for new sounds, and especially for new words.

If only a dictionary didn't cost so much! Every cent his father earned was needed to house, feed, and clothe nine Powells — the parents, Martha, Mary, Wes, seven-year-old Bram, five-year-old Lida, and the two babies, Nell and Walter.

Every spring Reverend Powell seeded several acres of corn and oats. He also planted a large vegetable garden. Then he left home to preach to the far-off settlers. They called him a *circuit rider* because he rode horseback to hold services in a wide area circling Jackson.

The older children tended the crops and looked after the cows, pigs, and chickens.

Their father returned in time to help with the harvest. During the winter he worked as a tailor, making men's clothing. Because he preached against keeping Negroes as slaves, many people would not pay their share of Reverend Powell's salary. Thus there never was money enough for a dictionary.

"Someday I'm going to have one," Wes promised himself. He was so hungry for learning that in the past year he had read *The Farmers' Almanac.* He had read a book titled *Why the Negro Should Be Free.* He had read The Holy Bible. All of it!

He had even memorized the Gospel of St. Luke. It was pages and pages long. Some of the words were real tongue-twisters. But he repeated them over and over until they rolled smoothly off his tongue. When his father returned, Wes surprised him by reciting the long Gospel from memory.

"Wonderful!" his father had praised him. "When you grow up, you'll make a fine minister." At least, that was what Reverend Powell hoped his oldest son would be. That

13

was why he had named him John Wesley Powell, after John Wesley, the founder of the Methodist faith.

While he was cleaning the barn, Wes had an idea. Why hadn't he thought of it before? He ran into the house, where his father was preparing a sermon.

"A dictionary would help me be a good minister, wouldn't it?" he asked hopefully. He waited.

"Not as much as reading your Bible."

"Oh," Wes sighed.

"Why such an unhappy look, Son?" Reverend Powell asked.

Mrs. Powell spoke up. "Wes is starved for books. He wants a dictionary more than anything. He really should have one, too. He asks so many questions I cannot begin to answer."

Reverend Powell stroked his bushy black beard. "Suppose you had a choice, Wes. Would you rather have a dictionary, or go to a real school?"

"A real school?" Wes looked up at his

14

father. He could hardly believe his own ears.

"Where? Here? In Jackson!" Martha and Mary exclaimed.

"May I go too?" Bram and Lida each asked.

"A real school, right here in Jackson," their father explained. "I heard about it only this morning. All the men are going to help build it tomorrow. The ladies are to bring a picnic lunch."

"Hooray! A picnic!" the children cried gleefully.

"Will we have readers?"

"I should say there will be readers, and slates, too. Our good friend Mr. Crookham is donating a big blackboard and a large colored map of the world, and —" Mr. Powell winked at Wes, "and a dictionary!"

CHAPTER 2

Sticks and Stones

Wes ran all the way to school that first day. He wore knee-length pants, a blue cotton pullover shirt, long black stockings, and buttoned shoes.

"May I play tag with you?" he asked several older boys chasing each other.

"Play with the little kids," they shouted at him. Wes was small for his age, with skinny arms and legs.

16

Just then, the teacher, Mr. Summers, rang the bell. The pupils raced to get into line.

"Beginners on this side. Older students over here," Mr. Summers called out. He was a nice-looking young man. The children called him Teacher.

Bram and Lida joined the beginners. Martha and Mary lined up with the older girls. They wore cotton dresses, long black stockings, and high buttoned shoes. They squealed when the big boys tried to crowd between them. The boys pulled their braids, and ducked to the end of the line.

Since he had shared lessons with his older sisters, Wes stood beside them. They teased him until he moved down with the older boys.

"Get in the beginners' line," they told him. One named Sam shoved Wes away. Wes didn't care. He was too happy to shove back. Anyway, the teacher would decide whether he should be with the beginners or the others.

One by one, the pupils stepped inside to

the teacher's desk. Bram and Lida only had to tell their names. They sat together on the "first reader" bench. There were no desks.

"Read this," Teacher said to the older pupils. They had to read a page from a book and write their names on the blackboard. Some could not do either. Others had to spell ten words and do simple arithmetic problems.

Martha and Mary did very well. They were sent to the older girls' bench. The older boys had another bench to themselves.

Wes was one of the last to be questioned. The teacher was surprised at the words Wes could spell and read. "You're no beginner. You're ahead of some of the oldest boys and girls. Take your place on the older boys' bench."

"Yes, sir!" Wes walked straight-backed to the bench. He was very proud.

"Teacher's pet!" Sam hissed when Wes tried to sit beside him. He and the others spread out so that there was no room for Wes.

"Boys!" Teacher warned.

When Wes inched onto the end of the bench, his feet dangled above the floor. Every time Mr. Summers's back was turned, Sam bumped him off. Wes said nothing.

At recess Wes tried to make friends with Sam and the older boys.

"Go away!" Sam said.

"Yeah, go away!" the others parroted Sam. He was bigger than all of them, and their ringleader.

"I don't have to."

"You do too."

"Who says so?" Wes demanded.

"If you know what's good for you, Smarty, stop answering all the questions. You make me look bad."

Wes eyed Sam. "You quit copying off my slate. If you paid attention, you could answer the questions."

Sam knocked Wes down. When he bounded to his feet, Sam pushed him again, and ran. After school Sam warned, "If you sit next to me tomorrow, I'll poke you in the nose."

The next morning Wes took his same place on the bench. When Sam swung at him, he ducked. Mr. Summers punished Sam by making him stand in the corner for fifteen minutes. That made Sam dislike Wes even more.

At recess Sam did punch Wes in the nose,

and it bled badly. This time the teacher
whipped Sam with a birch rod.

"My Pa will get you fired for this!" Sam
blubbered, and went home. He thought his
father was very important because he owned
a large farm and several slaves. But nothing
happened. Mr. Summers was not dismissed,

and Sam didn't bother Wes for a few days.

Wes was such a fine pupil that the teacher could not help favoring him. This made Sam and his friends angry. They tried whispering threats, to frighten Wes so much that he would stay away from school. But Wes just grinned at them. Then they called him nasty names during recess.

"Sticks and stones can break my bones, but names can never hurt me," Wes answered back.

Sam and his friends put their heads together and talked. When the school bell rang, they came into the schoolroom, looking pleased.

Wes was too busy reading about Christopher Columbus to notice. For a moment he closed his eyes. He dreamed he was an explorer, braving the dangers of the uncharted ocean. Then he opened his eyes, and went on with the story.

When school was dismissed that afternoon, Wes asked, "Teacher, may I stay and read some more?" He knew Mr. Summers always remained to prepare the lessons for the next day.

"Of course you may."

An hour later Wes closed the book. He had to hurry home to fill the wood box and milk the cows. But his footsteps lagged along the dusty path. His feet might have been on the ground, but his thoughts were sailing with Columbus. He did not see Sam and the others jump at him from behind a large oak tree.

"Where do you think you're going, Smarty?" Sam demanded.

"Home."

"That's what you think. You're going to get what's coming to you! You're not making us look like dummies any more!"

Sam pushed Wes so hard that he toppled back on the ground. But he bounded up and butted Sam in the stomach. Sam grunted, and pulled Wes's hair while the others kicked and slapped him. Wes fought like a small hornet. His nose and mouth began to bleed, and one eye puffed up. His shirt was torn.

"Holler quits!" Sam yelled at him, breathing hard. His face was scratched.

But Wes would not holler anything. He just kept on fighting.

Finally, one boy said, "Aw, let him go. He doesn't know when he's licked."

"You come back to school any more, and I'll beat you ten times worse than this," Sam said angrily.

"I'm coming to school every day. You can't stop me," Wes answered through swollen lips. He turned his back on the bullies and limped away.

Sam grabbed a rock and hit him in the back. The others pelted him with stones. But they could not make him cry or run.

When Wes stumbled into the kitchen, his parents were visiting with Mr. Crookham. His mother hurried for warm water and bandages. Reverend Powell tried to make Wes tell who had hurt him. Wes refused to say. It was Martha and Mary who told what a hard time he had been having at school.

"Sam won't pick on us because we're

24

girls. Bram and Lida are too little. Sam doesn't like Wes because he's so smart. And Sam dislikes all of us because Papa preaches that it's wrong to keep the Negroes as slaves, and his father is a slave holder."

Reverend Powell groaned. He preached against slavery because he thought it was wrong. But he felt bad that his young son suffered because of this.

"Wes simply cannot go back to school," Mrs. Powell said. "Look at this cut above his eye. Those awful bullies could have blinded him."

Mr. Powell agreed sadly. "All right, we will keep the lad home."

Wes cried out, "I won't stay home. I'm going back to school."

His mother burst into tears. "You can't." Yet she knew that her son must not be denied an education. "Whatever are we to do?"

"May I say something?" Mr. Crookham spoke up. He was a rich farmer who also spoke out against slavery. Because of this, the slave owners had threatened to burn his

25

house and crops. He had ignored their threats.

"I agree that it's too dangerous for Wes to return to school. A grown man has a fair chance to protect himself, but not a small lad." Then he reminded the Powells that he owned a fine library and museum. If Wes would like to come to his library for a few hours every day, he would teach him.

"When the weather is nice, we can go exploring up Salt Creek Gorge," he promised the young boy. "Would you like that?"

Wes could hardly believe the good news. He had visited Mr. Crookham's library. It was a fine log building on his farm. There were many shelves of wonderful books, and dozens of maps. There were lamps, a real desk, and a fireplace. Part of the library was a museum. It contained all sorts of things Wes loved: rocks, birds' nests, stuffed animals, and Indian relics.

"Yes!" he exclaimed, although it hurt to move his bruised lips. "May I start tomorrow?"

CHAPTER 3

The Biggest Man
in Ohio

Wes was waiting on the library steps when Crookham came from his house the next morning. A very fat man, he joked about being "the biggest man in Ohio." He greeted his pupil, "Well, you're the early bird. I thought most boys hated school."

"I don't," Wes told his new teacher. He helped build a fire in the fireplace.

Mr. Crookham lowered himself into an oversized chair. Wes sat on a high stool. On a table between them were maps and books. "Wes, what do you enjoy studying most?"

Wes blinked. His other teacher never asked the pupils what they liked. "Reading about men who went to faraway places, like Christopher Columbus." Then he added hastily, "I like spelling and arithmetic, but reading best."

"What do you know about earth science?"

"Earth science?" Wes had never heard about it. He knew almost nothing about the earth, and less about science, whatever *that* was.

Mr. Crookham knew Wes had a great ability to remember what he had read. But he felt that it was of little use unless Wes understood the meaning of the words and ideas he had read about. "The way I teach may be different from the way Mr. Summers taught, but don't worry. We will look into many new subjects. Since you're interested in explorers, let's talk about Columbus."

First Wes told what he had already learned about the discoverer of America.

"What Columbus did is only the bare bones of the story," Mr. Crookham pointed out.

He told what kind of man Columbus was, and what the Italian navigator tried to prove by sailing westward across unknown waters. He described the tall, sturdy man, his friends, and his ships, the *Pinta,* the *Nina,* and the *Santa Maria.* On a map he traced Columbus's three routes. He made sure Wes understood the reason for the daring undertaking, and the hardships that went with it.

For over an hour, Wes sat on the stool without fidgeting. Although the seat was hard and his back became weary, he did not complain.

Suddenly Mr. Crookham changed the subject. "Let's move about," he said as he heaved himself onto his feet. "What is this?" he asked, pointing to one of many stuffed animals and birds.

"That's easy. That's a squirrel."

"Close your eyes and describe it to me."

Wes did so, in a general way. When he opened his eyes, Mr. Crookham handed him the stuffed animal. He learned more by examining it closely: the feel of the fur, the

shape of the squirrel's head, ears, feet, and body. After that Mr. Crookham told Wes how this bushy-tailed member of the rodent order built its nest, fed, ranged over the countryside, and raised a family. The squirrel became much more real to Wes this way.

The teacher and the pupil moved on to examine a muskrat, a beaver, a field mouse, a water snake, a finch, a robin, and several butterflies. Wes knew all of these — what farm boy didn't? But he never had studied them closely before. He did not know their part in his own world of Jackson, Ohio. "It's no use yearning to go to faraway places until you know a great deal about the world near you," Mr. Crookham told Wes.

Next he pulled a large watch from his pocket. "My stars! It's noontime. Let's sit on the steps in the sunshine and have lunch. You must be starved."

He *was* hungry, Wes admitted. He had been too excited to eat more than a half bowl of mush that morning. Mrs. Crookham had packed a basket lunch for them.

Wes carried the basket to the steps. Mr. Crookham filled the entire doorsill. Wes perched on the step below. What a lunch! No wonder the farmer was big! There were a half dozen buns filled with cold meat and cheese, pickles, hard-boiled eggs, fresh sweet plums, and crisp, cinnamon-flavored cookies called *snickerdoodles.*

"Enjoying yourself?"

"Yes!" Wes beamed. He just hoped he could remember all the teacher had told him.

"You will forget some things," Mr. Crookham reminded him. "You can't swallow an apple pie in one gulp, can you? Well, learning is like an apple pie. To get the most out of it, you have to take it slowly, bite by bite."

Wes giggled. He had never heard learning compared to apple pie.

After lunch Mr. Crookham moved to the bookshelves. He showed Wes books about world history and American history, geography, poetry, plants, animals, and rocks. "We will dip into many of these," he promised.

Although Wes was only nine, Mr. Crookham read him passages from *The Decline and Fall of the Roman Empire,* by Gibbons. This was very difficult reading for a nine-year-old. However, Mr. Crookham explained about Rome, its people and history, and why it fell. Whenever he came to a difficult word, he stopped to explain it. He had Wes locate Rome on a large map, and trace the boundaries of the Roman Empire. Once more he told his pupil, "Don't worry if this seems too hard for you. We will repeat it all."

Wes was allowed to put the books back in their places on the shelves. In that way, he learned to shelve books properly, by the authors' last names.

"Had enough, young man? Tired?"

"Tired?" Wes laughed. He felt like turning handsprings.

Mr. Crookham chuckled. "All right, let's move about some more."

This time he directed Wes to several small boxes set on a tray. The boxes contained samples of sand, coal, iron ore, clay, soil, limestone, and rock salt.

"Most of these were gathered in Ohio," he explained. He had the young boy feel them, smell them, and taste them. Then he told him how he thought the earth had come into being billions of years ago. He described how the earth's surface was shaped by the action of water, wind, and earthquakes. He said that soil was made from rocks which had been broken down into countless small pieces.

"Every rock has a fascinating story," he said. "Someday you will want to know these stories. Now look at this piece of limestone. It was formed when tiny shells piled up on the sea bottom."

This was John Wesley Powell's first introduction to geology (*jee ol' oh jih*). Mr. Crookham explained that geology is the science dealing with the beginning, change, and shape of the earth's surface. Wes listened, open-mouthed. "This isn't just dirt. It's ge-ol-o-gy!" He repeated the new word. "Tell me some more about geology."

"Tomorrow," Mr. Crookham promised.

He knew Wes had to be home in time to chop stove wood and help milk the cows.

As Wes skipped home across the fields and through the trees, he pretended he was an explorer, like Columbus.

Maybe he could explore unknown places, too, someday.

CHAPTER 4

A New Idea About Indians

The next day Mr. Crookham retold some of the story about Columbus. He read several more pages from the book about the Roman Empire. He tested Wes on the differences between sand, clay, coal, and other rocks. He showed Wes some tiny sea shells. "I found these on the banks of the Ohio River twenty-five miles from here," he said.

"How did they get there?" Wes knew the river was a long way from the ocean.

Mr. Crookham explained that long, long ago a sea had covered what was now Ohio. Many sea animals had lived and died on its muddy bottom. When the sea withdrew, the shells became buried in the mud, and in time turned into stone.

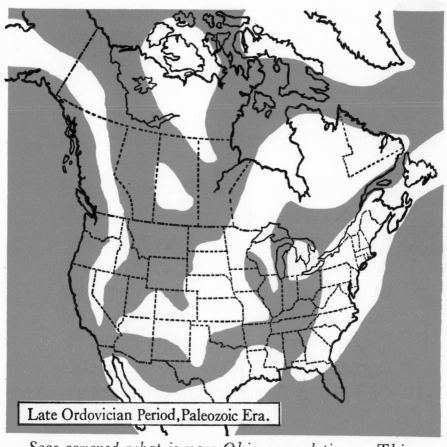

Late Ordovician Period, Paleozoic Era.

Seas covered what is now Ohio several times. This map shows North America 350,000,000 years ago.

Wes frowned. That must have happened long before he was born on March 24, 1834. It was hard to imagine so long a time. Sometimes he could not remember what had happened one month, or one year ago.

"I wish I could find some shells. I'd like to collect them. I want a collection all my own," Wes said.

"That's a good idea," his teacher agreed. "Someday soon, we'll go to Salt Creek Gorge and gather shells. We'll have a natural history excursion."

"Natural history excursion?" Wes repeated, stammering a little. "Is that like a picnic?"

A natural history excursion was a nature walk and picnic rolled into one. They would ride to Salt Creek Gorge in Mr. Crookham's buggy, and then walk along the creek there. On the way, Wes could point out the different trees, shrubs, birds, and insects. "And there is something we can dig for there," Mr. Crookham added. He moved to another table. On it, neatly arranged, were Indian relics —

stone bowls and clubs, red clay pipes, arrowheads, and parts of moccasins, clothing, and woven mats.

Wes shivered. "I hate Indians." He had heard many tales of Indians killing the white people who settled the frontiers of New York and Ohio. Sometimes wandering Indians passed through Jackson. Even though they were harmless, the townspeople drove them away.

Mr. Crookham scolded, "If you understood Indians, you would never say you hated them. You are speaking out of ignorance. That is very, very bad, Wes, whether it is about Indians or anything. I think we should have a talk about Indians right now." He walked over to a big chair by the fireplace.

"Didn't anyone ever tell you, Wes, that Indians are fine people?"

Wes shook his head. He had never heard anyone say anything good about Indians. Everyone on the frontier said the same thing: the only good Indian was a dead Indian. Wes repeated the saying.

Mr. Crookham became excited. "Don't you know that the Indians were living in North America long before the white men came? Don't you know that the white men took away the Indians' lands, and killed off the wild game they needed for food and clothing? No wonder the Indians fought the white men. If they were cruel or savage, it was because the Indians didn't know any better. They fought bitterly because they did not want to be robbed or conquered. But we — that is, the white men — outnumbered the Indians. We had better weapons. In time we did conquer them, at least the tribes in the eastern half of the United States."

Wes listened, wide-eyed. He had never thought about how the white settlers had treated the Indians. Until his teacher told him, he didn't know that Indians had languages all their own, many fine skills, and their own music and art legends.

Mr. Crookham talked on and on. He told his pupil about the Erie tribe which had once roamed the south shore of Lake Erie; about the Shawnees from down South; about the Delawares from Pennsylvania. All these tribes had moved into Ohio after the white men took over their hunting grounds. Now they and the Ohio Indians were reduced to small bands of beggars.

Wes burst into tears. The poor Indians! They were worse off than the Negroes.

Wes's tears upset his teacher. "Pshaw, I didn't mean to make you cry." He dried Wes's cheeks. "All I wanted was to help you understand Indians a little better. I don't want you to be afraid of them. Be kind to them whenever you have the chance. Try to help them." Mr. Crookham mopped his face and sighed. "Someone will have to help them, someday."

"I'll try," Wes promised, so his teacher would feel better.

Mr. Crookham pushed himself out of his chair. He walked back to the table. He handed Wes a worn moccasin. "Think of having to make your own shoes, Wes. Sup-

41

pose you wanted to cut down a tree, but had no axe? Or chop stove wood, but had no hatchet? Imagine your mother trying to sew with a thorn for a needle, and animal sinew for thread. Think how much work went into making just one arrowhead."

As Wes looked at the bits of bone, leather, and stone, he saw them no longer as raggle-taggle leftovers. The moccasin was small enough to fit him. What was the Indian boy like who had worn it? What had become of him?

In only two days, Wes's teacher had opened his eyes to many new, wonderful things. Why, he would be an old man before he learned half enough, or visited the new places he was finding on maps, or earned enough money to buy a library full of books, or collected articles for a museum. He spoke these wishes aloud.

"I'll never have what I want. Papa isn't a rich farmer like you. Papa doesn't even have enough money to buy me a dictionary."

What Mr. Crookham said then really sur-

prised Wes. "There isn't anything in the whole world you can't have, if you really want it — particularly an education, and books, and a collection for a museum."

Wes's mouth gaped. He couldn't believe that.

"Let's talk about it while we sit on the steps and have lunch," Mr. Crookham suggested. The whole morning had flown by. Outside, the golden October sun was warm. Robins chirped at them. Sparrows and squirrels darted greedily for the crumbs Wes tossed toward them.

Mr. Crookham talked slowly. He didn't want Wes to forget what he said. "Wes, if you really want an education, you can get one. If you want books, you can have those, too. If you want to travel to faraway places, you can do that. You can, if you have patience. You can, if you never let hard work, or a lack of money, or delays discourage you.

"Right this moment you want to collect shells, and maybe Indian relics. Next week you might want to do something different.

You and I will talk about many more new things in the coming weeks. Maybe you'll discover something you like much better. Right now you think you want to be an explorer, like Christopher Columbus. Fine. But don't forget how hard Columbus had to struggle to reach his goal. Remember how few men of his time believed as he did? Remember what he had to give up to make his dream come true — what hardships and disappointments he suffered? It wasn't easy, was it?"

Wes shook his head.

"But Columbus made his dream come true, didn't he?"

Wes nodded. Even poverty hadn't licked Christopher Columbus.

CHAPTER 5

Wes Starts
a "Museum"

A few days later, Mr. Crook-
ham told Wes, "We should have that natural
history excursion before the weather turns
cold. Can you be here an hour earlier tomorrow?"

Wes nodded. He would get up in the
middle of the night, if he had to. He couldn't
wait to go on his first nature walk. When he
reached the library the next morning, Mr.

Crookham and another man already were seated in the buggy.

"This is Dr. William Mather," Mr. Crookham told Wes. "He's Ohio's first State Geologist. We've been friends for many years. What I know about geology I learned from him."

Dr. Mather was thin, and wore a baggy tweed suit. He was smoking a red clay pipe. It was like some of the pipes in Mr. Crookham's Indian collection.

Wes was puzzled. He had heard of farmers and preachers and storekeepers. But he had never heard of a State Geologist. After he squeezed onto the buggy seat, he asked Dr. Mather, "Do you have a job picking up rocks?"

Both men laughed heartily. Dr. Mather answered, "Yes, I do have a job picking up rocks. Very special rocks.

"You see, Wes, Ohio needs to know where there is coal which can be mined, and good clay for making pottery, and sandstone strong enough for buildings. It is my job to find these 'rocks.' I map the area of each deposit. I also draw maps of big sections of Ohio. That way, farmers know where the soil is good, and road builders know where the ground is firm. The state pays me to do this, so that Ohio will prosper."

"Oh." Wes had no idea geology could be useful. "Do you have to sleep outdoors all by yourself?"

"Yes. I have a wagon in which I carry a tent, camping gear, a shotgun, and some food. I also carry tools: a sledge hammer for breaking up big rocks, a hand hammer, a shovel, a steel wedge, and some chisels. During the daylight hours I walk, and make notes on what I see. And I collect samples of rocks. At night, by firelight, I label these rocks, and store them in small sacks. I also keep a big notebook called a journal."

"Isn't it kind of cold working outside in the winter time?" Wes wondered aloud.

"Oh, in winter time I work in a warm office. That's when I draw maps and write my reports. But from early spring to late

fall, I travel all over Ohio. I have slept outdoors many, many times."

"Alone?"

"Oh, yes."

"Did you ever run into any bears?"

"Lots of times."

"And Indians?"

"Oh my, yes! I've camped with Indians
many times. They're fine people."

Dr. Mather had camped with Indians, and
he still had his scalp. Maybe there was some
truth in what Mr. Crookham said.

Finally they arrived at Salt Creek Gorge.
A small stream trickled along the bottom of
the ravine. Wes jumped from the buggy and
ran to the water's edge. He skipped pebbles
across the stream.

"Did you know a pebble was once part of
a bigger rock?" Dr. Mather asked him.

Wes nodded. "Mr. Crookham told me
that."

"But I didn't tell him how big rocks are
worn down into pebbles," Mr. Crookham
said. "You tell him."

Dr. Mather told Wes that the solid part of the earth's crust was made of rock. Rain and frost, cold and heat broke up the solid rock. The big pieces washed into creeks and rivers. As the water rushed over them, the big pieces bumped into each other. They broke into smaller rocks. The smaller rocks tumbled against each other until their edges were worn smooth. They also wore on each other until they became smaller and smaller, as small as grains of sand. Meanwhile, the rocks and sand ground the creek bottom or river channel deeper and deeper. Soon the water ran deeper and deeper below the surface. Its banks were two feet high, or ten feet, or a hundred, or even a thousand feet high. It all depended on how long and how hard the rocks, sand, and the water wore away the stream bed.

"That is how Salt Creek Gorge was formed," Mr. Crookham added.

Wes followed his two teachers upstream slowly. Salt Creek had little water in it that time of year. The banks rose higher.

"Did you know the banks of a stream are like pages of a book?" Dr. Mather asked. "They tell a story. See, these banks are made of limestone. If you look closely, you can see tiny pieces of shells in it." Dr. Mather picked up a piece. He tapped it lightly with his hand hammer. It broke into several pieces. Inside was a small, perfect shell.

Wes got so excited that he scrambled up and down the banks, stuffing his pockets with pretty rocks. He wrapped several shells in his handkerchief.

Mr. Crookham smiled. "See how easy it is to start a collection? Now, when you get home, label each rock and shell. Mark what each is if you can; in this case, the rock is limestone. Under *Limestone,* write *Salt Creek Gorge, Ohio.* That way you'll always know what each rock is, and where it was found."

Dr. Mather agreed. "That's what you do when you collect for a real museum."

"I won't forget," Wes promised. Already he had visions of the shelves in his bedroom loaded with rocks and shells.

"Let me warn you," Dr. Mather said later on. "Always be careful when you're climbing over loose rocks. You wouldn't want to break an ankle or trigger a rock slide. And never dig at the bottom of a cliff where there are rocks hanging over your head. Watch out for deserted well diggings covered with brush. And don't use a hammer in such a way that chips fly off and hit you in the face."

"Yes, sir. I'll try to remember."

After a picnic lunch, Mr. Crookham drove to an Indian burial ground. There Wes found a few old beads and some arrowheads. On the way home he said, "I don't know which I like best, digging for rocks or for Indian relics."

Mr. Crookham chuckled. "You have many years in which to decide what you want to do."

"Oh, I have to be a preacher. Papa says so," Wes told his friend.

That was not all Reverend Powell had decided, Wes soon found out. His father objected to the hours Wes spent building his collection. He called the rocks and shells, birds' nests, cocoons, and dried plants "trash."

"I don't approve of your studying science," Reverend Powell said sternly. "You're going to be a minister."

Wes didn't know what to do. He loved his father. He didn't want to displease him.

Fortunately, Wes's mother promised, "I'll see that Wes does not neglect his Bible studies. But surely there is nothing wrong in his knowing more about God's wonderful world."

After that, Wes divided his study time equally between the Bible and his collections. Every trip to the barn, or the pasture, or Crookham's farm became a nature walk. He learned something new every day. His mother helped him make a net for catching insects. Trying to catch insects taught him to be quiet and patient. He learned to observe what he had never noticed before: the color of tree bark, the shapes of leaves, the tell-tale tracks of animals. Since he shared the second-story bedroom with his younger brother, he taught Bram many things. He even let Bram help with his "museum." All the objects were crowded on the window sill and wall shelves, and even in boxes under Wes's bed.

Wes continued going to school at Crook-ham's. There were no classes during the spring planting season, nor at harvest time. As he grew older, Wes did harder work on the family farm, such as plowing. He grew strong, but not very tall.

The town of Jackson was also growing. More and more southerners came to live there. Still Reverend Powell did not stop preaching against the wrong of slavery. Mr. Crookham traveled over the countryside too, talking against it. This took real courage because both men were often threatened with bodily harm. One day a mob in Jackson gathered to tar and feather them. Loyal friends helped them escape.

Another day, at breakfast, the Powells were startled to hear someone pounding on the door.

"That's Mr. Crookham's voice!" Wes cried out. He opened the kitchen door.

"A mob set fire to my library!" he told the Powells. "All my books and maps have gone up in flames. Everything in the museum was destroyed!"

After Mr. Crookham calmed down, he said sadly, "I'm afraid there will be no more school sessions, Wes."

"Couldn't I help you gather another collection? You may have mine for a starter."

Mr. Crookham sighed. "No, it's no use. I'm too old to start all over again. But you won't give up, will you? You will keep on studying and collecting?"

"Oh, yes!" Wes promised. But in his heart, Wes was sick. There would be no more lessons at Crookham's. He could not attend the Jackson school. He guessed his school days were over forever.

CHAPTER 6

"Where Could I Buy a Book?"

In the summer of 1846, Reverend Powell decided to move to Wisconsin.

Wes was thrilled. At last he was going to a faraway place. To an Ohio lad, Wisconsin was the frontier. There were Indians still roaming the forests up there. It was still a territory, not yet admitted to statehood.

"How do we get to Wisconsin?" he asked his father.

"By horse and wagon, of course. We'll take all our furniture with us. We'll need two carriages and a wagon. I'm counting on you to handle one of the teams."

For days, the Powell household was in an uproar. The house and land were sold. The children helped pack the wagon. Wes discovered there was no room for his collection. For a brief moment he felt bad. Then he reminded himself, "I can start a new one in Wisconsin." He saved only a few choice rocks and shells.

The hardest part of leaving was saying good-by to George Crookham. Now that he was twelve, Wes would have been ashamed to cry. So he stammered to his friend, "I don't know how to thank you for the things you did for me."

"Our country needs scientists, Wes. If you go to college and become a scientist, that will be thanks enough. I've given you a good start. The rest is up to you. I'm expecting great things of you, lad."

Wes extended his hand in a farewell clasp.

"I'm going to miss you something awful! I'll do my best, sir. G- good-by." He hurried away before tears spilled down his cheeks.

The Powells settled in southernmost Wisconsin, in Walworth County. Their home there was a one-story shack. Behind the shack was a weed-choked garden. There was a creek flashing like a silver ribbon across the clearing and beyond it, many oak trees.

It was really not much different from Ohio.

In the spring the older children helped their father plant corn and oats and a large vegetable garden. Then Reverend Powell announced, "Tomorrow I shall leave to minister to the far outlying districts. I shall not return until fall. Wes, I'm placing you in charge of the farm. It's up to you to see that we have a good crop."

Mrs. Powell objected. "Wes is too young to have all that on his shoulders."

Wes said nothing. He had been brought up to obey his father. He would not think of complaining. Mr. Powell did not ask his son if the task was too great. He departed the next day, confident that his wishes would be fulfilled.

Wes worked so hard that he had little energy left over for growing. But as plants sprouted, and birds and insects reappeared, he started a new collection. There were no really interesting rocks around the farm, and so for the time he forgot about geology. By summer's end, he had a fine display of insects. He made his own wooden pins and mounting boards.

His mother gave him constant encouragement. "I know something will work out so that you can have more schooling. Papa means for you to go to college someday."

The Powells had no wheat or corn to market the first year. But the second fall, the family cleared nearly sixty acres for planting, and there was enough grain left to sell. When harvest time the third year was approaching,

Mrs. Powell received word from her husband that this year he could not get home in time to help. "Well, I guess it's up to us," she told the children.

Wes wasn't worried. He had helped with many harvests. He planned carefully. The oats must be cut and threshed first, then the wheat. The corn was to be picked last. The work was so hard that sometimes Wes fell exhausted to the ground. But after a nap, he rose and resumed working. The bigger the crop, the more money the family would have. Maybe there would be enough to buy a dictionary or some other books.

When the crops were ready for market, Reverend Powell still had not returned.

Mrs. Powell worried. "We must sell our grain. But we can't leave the farm and all go to market," she said.

"I'll go," Wes offered. Southport, the nearest settlement, was four days' travel. "Bram, can you do my chores while I'm gone?"

"You bet," Bram answered. He was as tall as his older brother now, and very sturdy.

Mrs. Powell explained to Wes how he must bargain for a good price for the crops. She gave him a list of things to buy. She made him a money belt to wear under his clothing. "If I get a good price for the wheat, may I buy a book?" he asked hopefully.

"If it doesn't cost too much. You deserve something special for all you have done."

Wes left at dawn. Having nothing to do but drive a wagon was a real treat. He whistled at birds and squirrels. He made a wreath of purple asters to wear on his straw hat. At night he pulled off into a thicket and slept soundly.

Although there were fewer than two hundred people in Southport, Wes thought of it as a big city. He located the grain buyer and obtained a fair price for the crop. He hid most of the money in his belt before he went shopping. He bought everything on the list: groceries, spices, two bolts of checkered cloth, needles, thread, and knitting wool. But there were no books for sale.

A storekeeper advised him to check the farmers' booths.

After the wagon was loaded, Wes walked around. Many farmers' wives were selling preserves, quilts, eggs, and hand-loomed cloth. But none offered books for sale. So Wes started asking strangers, "Where could I buy a book?"

Most shrugged. They didn't know. But one young man asked, "What kind of book are you looking for?"

"I really want a second-hand dictionary, or a book on plants and insects."

The young man smiled. "I have some books in my wagon. I'll show them to you."

On the way to the wagon, the young man said, "My name's Bill Wheeler. What's yours?"

Wes told him about himself as they walked to the wagon.

"Here they are," Bill said. He pulled a box from under the seat. Wes smiled when he saw a copy of Eaton's *Manual of Botany*. He sat down and thumbed through it.

Bill was puzzled. Wes looked like any other barefoot, sunburned farm lad. Most such boys had little education. "Where did you learn about botany?" he asked.

Wes was glad to have someone to talk to. He told Bill about George Crookham's library and museum. He also told him about his own collection. "Someday I'm going to college," he said stoutly.

"I've been to college. Next month I take my teacher examination at Janesville. If I pass, I'll be teaching school somewhere out here."

"You've been to college! Tell me what it's like," Wes begged.

Hours passed as the two, one twenty and the other fifteen, talked. Bill told Wes, "Almost all the fellows in college were taking at least one class in chemistry and one in geology."

Wes had almost forgotten about the subject of geology. He told Bill about his excursion with Dr. Mather.

The two cooked their supper and continued to talk. "Let me lend you some books," Bill offered. "I really don't want to sell them. Here, take this botany text, and this one on entomology (*en toh mol' oh jih*). It's all about insects, and will help you identify them. And here are two on advanced mathematics and grammar. You may have this magnifying glass, too."

"How will I return them to you?" Wes asked as he hugged the books tightly.

Bill laughed. "When I get tired of my own cooking, I'll ride over to your farm. Would that be all right?"

"Of course!"

Wes read almost all the way home.

He did not mind missing school another winter, now that he had good books to study. At first Reverend Powell objected to the science books. But he gave in when Wes said, "Bill Wheeler said I have to pass a general science test before I can go to college. If I don't pass it, I'll have to study science there."

The Reverend fumed. In his school days,

nobody wasted time studying science. "See
that you pass that test beforehand. I'm not
spending money to have you study science in
college. You are to train to be a minister."

"I know," Wes answered, a little unhap-
pily. He was beginning to doubt that he
wanted to be a minister at all. But of course
he would not dare disobey his father.

Several weeks later, Bill Wheeler visited
the farm. The girls admired him because he
was so handsome and gentlemanly. Reverend Powell questioned Bill about his religion
and habits. He could not find anything
wrong with him.

Wes could hardly wait to show Bill his collection. "What do you think of it?" he asked eagerly.

Bill looked at the large, neat display. "Say, this beetle collection is excellent! Keep this up, and someday you'll have a display in a university."

Wes blushed. "I'm only a beginner."

"But you're getting better all the time," Bram interrupted. He told Bill, "Wes is teaching me, so I can go to college too."

Wes sighed. "I wish college didn't cost so much. Papa says the tuition at some schools runs as high as a hundred dollars a year."

"And we both can't be spared from farm chores," Bram added.

"Then do this — Wes, you study until you can pass your teacher examination. By that time, Bram will be able to do your chores. You can teach a four-month country school. Save the money you make teaching, and go to college one semester. Work here on the farm in the summers. When Walter is old enough to do the heavy work, Bram, you can teach and go to college. Then both of you work, and pay a hired man, so that Walter can go to college. That's the way my brothers and I did it. It can be done, if you don't mind stringing out the time."

Wes and Bram looked at each other. They wouldn't mind that. They would be glad to help each other, and Walter, through college.

That evening everybody gathered about the parlor organ to sing. Wes saw Bill gazing at Mary, and Mary looking shyly back at him. Wes had a hunch that Bill Wheeler would call again.

Often months passed between Bill's visits. He taught school, then returned to college. He began to court Mary.

It wasn't long after Wes's sixteenth birthday that Bill Wheeler and Mary Powell were married. Martha was married soon after. Wes wondered how his mother could get along without his sisters' help. When he saw Nell and Lida take over, he asked Bram, "After harvest time, could you and Walter do without me?"

"You bet," Bram said. He was taller and stronger than Wes now.

That fall Bram took the crops to market. When Reverend Powell returned in October, Wes had made up his mind. "Father, I want to prepare for college. I can't do it all on my own at home. I have to go to school somewhere first."

To Wes's surprise, his father agreed. "You've been very patient, Son. I'll give you enough money to go to school. After you pass your entrance tests, I'll pay your tuition to Oberlin College, in Ohio."

Oberlin! It was one of the finest in America.

"Of course, I expect you to study for the ministry," his father went on.

"But you know I don't want to. You know I want to be a scientist."

"You'll get over that nonsense."

Wes prayed for patience. He had tried for so long to convince his father that he meant to be a scientist, and that science was not "nonsense." "I'm sorry, Father. I will not study for the ministry. You had a divine calling to preach. I haven't had."

"You will do as I say," the Reverend said sharply. "Either that, or I will not give you one cent toward your college expenses."

Wes dragged to his room. He sat at his homemade desk. He put his head down. Then he took a good look at his hands. They were the work-calloused hands of a man. For four years he had struggled to educate himself. Although he did not want to disobey his father, he had to. He was determined to be something more than a farmer.

He prayed hard, asking for help.

The next morning he appeared with his few clothes and books wrapped in a pack.

Wes said good-by to his family. Then he shouldered his pack and walked out of the clearing. For the first few miles he felt lonely. Then excitement welled up in him. A marvelous new world of learning and adventure beckoned him onward.

CHAPTER 7

The Coffee-
Colored
Mississippi

W_{es} walked almost twenty
miles that golden October day. By nightfall
he reached a farm about two miles from
Janesville, Wisconsin. He knocked on the
kitchen door.

"I was hoping you could use some help
mornings and evenings, in exchange for
board and room," he said to the farmer in
the doorway.

"Why can't you work during the day?" the farmer asked, so that he would have more time to study Wes.

"I want to be free to go to school in town, and prepare myself for college."

The farmer rubbed his chin. He could use help, and he thought Wes looked like a real worker. "Any experience tending cattle and sheep?"

"Oh, yes, sir. I was brought up on a farm."

The man was satisfied. He promised Wes could be free during the day to attend school and study. "By the time you chop some kindling, supper will be ready," he smiled.

Several days later, Wes started back to school in a one-room building in Janesville. He didn't feel out of place. Several other boys were taller than he was. But the teacher was young, and poorly prepared. At first Wes was disappointed. Then he told himself, "At least I'm going to school again."

He soon discovered he needed a great deal of work in grammar and mathematics in order to get into college. He studied very hard, often by firelight. Sometimes he missed his family so much that he almost gave up to return home. But he learned to overcome his homesickness by doing extra homework.

In the fall of 1851, Wes was surprised to receive a letter from his father. Reverend Powell reported that he had sold the farm. He was moving the family onto three hundred and twenty acres of rough land near Bonus Prairie, Illinois. He wanted Wes to drop his schooling and put the new farm in good order.

For a moment, Wes was angry. How could his father expect him to give up his studies? But when he thought of his brothers and sisters breaking the sod and planting without his help, he knew he could not let them down. With an aching heart, he packed his books. Once more he helped his family move to a new home. Once more he took full responsibility for managing the farm.

He was not unhappy. He loved his mother and the younger children. While Nell and Lida washed dishes and Bram strained the

milk, Wes read to them. He made meal time lively with word games and spell-downs. And every night he studied mathematics and grammar.

After the crops were harvested, his father again offered to pay Wes's tuition to Oberlin if he would study for the ministry.

For a brief moment Wes was tempted. Then his back stiffened. "No, thank you, Father."

"How are you ever going to earn money enough for college expenses?" his father demanded impatiently.

"I'll think of something."

Wes thought, but no workable ideas came to him. He prayed hard. He told God that he wanted to be a scientist. Since his faith was very strong, Wes felt sure his prayer would be answered.

A new idea came to him. Why not take the teacher examination now? He was positive that he knew as much as, if not more than, the teacher in Janesville. If he passed, he could teach, save his money, and put himself through college!

Wes had to walk thirty miles on a frozen, rutted road to Jefferson County, Wisconsin, to take the test. The school superintendent who gave the test asked him questions which he was permitted to answer aloud. He liked young Wes so much that he invited him to have dinner and stay overnight. Just before Wes went to bed, the kindly man signed a certificate stating that John Wesley Powell was prepared to teach school.

"But I thought I'd have to take written tests too," Wes stammered.

"Most would-be schoolmasters do, but you have prepared yourself so well that I'm willing to pass you without the written tests. Congratulations, young man. I think you have the makings of a fine schoolmaster. Since you have never taught school before, I can offer you only a country school. The salary is fourteen dollars a month. You will live and eat with the families who have children attending your school."

"I can't thank you enough," Wes said gratefully. He almost turned cartwheels, but he remembered in time that a schoolmaster-to-be must act grown-up.

The next morning Wes hurried to open

his one-room school, near the superintendent's house. There were no desks. The pupils sat on split logs. A board nailed to the wall served as his "desk." From a farmer's wife he borrowed a broom, a mop, and cleaning rags. He scrubbed away the dirt and cobwebs. There were no maps, no dictionary, no reference books. But there were schoolbooks, tablets, and pencils. Although he was only seventeen and a half years old, he was determined to be a fine schoolmaster.

The following day the farm children from miles around reported to the school. "Good morning, Teacher!" they sang out.

Teacher . . . Wes thought it was wonderful to be called that. It made all his hours of study worthwhile.

The older boys had planned to make life miserable for Teacher. Instead, they found themselves liking him. He wasn't a stranger. He didn't act different. He was a farm lad who spoke their language. His hands were rough and calloused like theirs, his clothes threadbare, his face deeply tanned. During recess he pitched a fast ball. When they started calling him Mister Powell, Wes knew he had won them over.

Wes taught grades one through six. The sixth graders had lessons in elementary geometry, advanced grammar, geography, and American history.

Wes remembered George Crookham's way of teaching. He helped the pupils act out the story of Christopher Columbus.

"Let's do some more," they begged. Wes had them act out Washington crossing the Delaware and other important events.

One spring day in 1852, Wes led his pupils on a natural history excursion. He started them gathering plants, rocks, flowers, and insects for a school museum. Then some young adults asked, "Professor Powell, would you hold night classes for us? We want to study the great writers and poets. We also would like to know about this new-fangled thing called irrigation."

Professor! Wes felt ten years older, instead of barely eighteen. If folks were going to call him Professor, he must act like one. He stood as tall as possible.

"I will be glad to hold adult night classes," he agreed. How hard he must study to keep ahead of this class! But he was glad to have the chance of being with people his own age.

That spring was one of the happiest in Wes's life. He made many friends. He went on hay rides, to socials, to taffy pulls, and to dinners. The only dark spot in the picture was his not being able to save any money. The first few dollars he tucked away were spent on a dictionary. The next few went for science books.

But he refused to be glum. He had plenty of offers to work as a hired man that summer. "I'll save that money for school," he determined.

But in the late spring, he received another letter from his father. Reverend Powell wrote that he was planning to sell the Bonus Prairie farm after the crops were in. He wanted to move the entire family to Wheaton, Illinois, a few miles west of Chicago. A new college would open there soon. If Wes would come home, he would pay him the wages of a hired man. And if Wes would help move the family, his father would pay his tuition at the new Illinois Institute.

Wes read and reread the letter. His father said nothing about his having to study for the ministry. Wes couldn't believe his good luck. As soon as the school semester ended, he hurried home. Once more he took over management of the farm. By November, the Powells were settled in their new home.

In December, Illinois Institute opened its doors to elementary, high school, and college students. Six Powells reported for enrollment.

When the man in charge of enrolling students handed Wes the list of courses offered, he almost grabbed it. He scanned it eagerly. Then he had a sickening disappointment. "Surely this isn't all! May I please see the list of courses on advanced mathematics and science?"

"I'm sorry," the man replied. "We aren't

offering those subjects. All you can take are those for teacher training or the ministry."

Wes had to clench his fists to keep from crying out. There was not a single course offered that he had not already covered on his own. He stumbled out of the building. For hours he tramped about in the cold. What could he do? He had no money saved. He would not go back to being a hired man.

But the longer he walked, the more his disappointment wore off. "What am I moping about?" he asked himself angrily. "I can go back to teaching, and this time really save money."

In 1854 Wes began teaching at the Emerson School, on Long Creek, east of Decatur, Illinois. He earned twenty-four dollars a month. By 1855 he had money enough to enroll in the science department of Illinois College, at Jacksonville, in the west central part of the state.

At first Wes was shy. He thought everyone was smarter than he. His clothes were still threadbare. He wasn't tall, or handsome.

He combed his hair up off his forehead, to appear taller. He wished his big, round nose weren't always so red. But shyness gave way to enthusiasm for his science courses. His classmates liked him because he was friendly and helpful.

The months slipped by swiftly and happily. As he watched the trees bud, Wes grew restless. Instead of paying attention in class, he watched clouds drifting by. He thought about the exciting vacations his friends were planning.

"I'm going on a walking tour out West," one told him.

"I'm going to gather shells along the Ohio River," another said.

"I'm going to Louisiana, to collect butterflies," said still another.

Wes sighed inwardly. "If only I could travel to some new region," he thought. As a youngster, he had wanted to be an explorer. Now he had almost forgotten how to explore and collect.

After class, he wandered through the

woods. He knew nearly every plant and small animal, the *flora* and *fauna,* as the professor called them. His family no longer farmed, and he was not needed at home. He was free to travel. "There must be something exciting I can do," he told himself.

But what?

One of his professors had told him that little had been written about the *flora* and *fauna* of the Mississippi River. Why couldn't he explore the great river, and do some of the collecting he had once loved to do? If he did some private teaching until June, he could earn the money needed for a summer's expenses.

The day school closed, Wes headed west. In a canvas knapsack he carried extra cloth-

ing, soap, a towel, a waterproof matchbox, and tent cloth. Wrapped in a rag were a small hand hammer, tweezers, his magnifying glass, and a knife. He included several text-books, many tablets, and pencils. A forty-mile walk brought him to the river about opposite Hannibal, Missouri.

"Ho! The Mississippi!" he shouted, see-ing the broad, beautiful river.

Several days later, he bought a leaky row-

boat, repaired it, and whittled new oars. He fashioned a weathertight locker for storing insects. He made a plant press of thin boards held together with cords. He fixed himself a *vasculum,* a hollow metal object attached to shoulder straps. A vasculum was used to

VASCULUM

INSECT LOCKER

carry plants until they were mounted. Wes spent a few of his coins on corn meal, beans, salt, tea, and bacon.

"Shall I go upstream, or downstream?" He tossed a coin. "Upstream it is!"

Wes pushed out from the grassy shoreline.

He rowed upstream. He filled his lungs with flower-fragrant air. There wasn't a happier man in the world.

About four o'clock every morning, the mist along the river began to lift.

Birds spiraled upward, seeking the sun. Larks, finches, and red-winged blackbirds chattered in the brush. As the sun rose, a lemon-yellow light swept over trees and water. Wes watched, silent, as gray moths hid under the leaves. Deer blended into thickets when flowers turned their faces to the sun. With oars upraised, he watched and marveled.

A chill morning or hot midday was the best time for catching insects. A morning after an evening thunderstorm was best for catching butterflies, he learned. He never failed to gasp at their bright, fragile beauty. From crumbling banks he gathered new shells and rocks. He watched robins carol the sunset from atop the highest trees. When the river's sheen dulled, when shadows covered the brush, he spied on raccoons, beavers, muskrats, and deer. But many nights when the gentle moths ventured forth, and bats squeaked overhead, he was already asleep.

Soon he rowed beyond the low-lying mud flats. He came onto picturesque rock bluffs soaring three hundred feet above the water. Opposite Davenport, Iowa, he found the muddy river banks had changed to limestone. A treasure house of shells was there.

Farther and farther upriver he rowed. He lived on fish, rabbit, and corn meal. He waved at men aboard steamboats and barges, at laborers working on the levees, at fishermen. Finally he reached St. Paul, Minnesota, over five hundred miles above his starting point. By selling his boat, he obtained money enough to mail his *flora* and *fauna* collection home.

After that, he walked across northern Wisconsin until he reached the upper part of Lake Michigan.

He marveled at this largest body of fresh water lying entirely within the United States. The water seemed so blue, after the coffee-colored Mississippi. The eastern shore was so far away that he couldn't even see it. He picked up many shells and rocks as he continued southward to Chicago. Finally he returned on foot to his home at Wheaton.

"Anybody home?" he called out as he entered the house.

Lida came running. "Wes! You're back!"

The others flocked around him, eager to hear about his experiences. That night his mother cooked a huge dinner. "You're so thin!" she exclaimed.

Wes was thin, and very sun-browned. His clothing was almost in rags, and his hair needed cutting. He didn't care. "I've had the most wonderful summer of my life," he told his family.

For three more summers John Wesley Powell rowed up or down the Mississippi River and the streams that flowed into it. During the school term, he attended college and taught school. But when the birds returned each spring, he sought nature's classroom out of doors.

Reverend Powell did not approve of his son's "wandering around." "You're twenty-four years old," his father told him. "You should settle down to some sort of steady job."

"I'm not just wandering around," Wes assured him. Slowly he was building one of the largest, most complete collections of fresh-water shells in the country. He was also saving enough money, coin by coin, to pay his tuition at Oberlin College.

In the fall of 1858, he told his father proudly, "I've been accepted as an advanced student at Oberlin, and I can pay my own way."

"You still plan to be a scientist?"

"More than ever," Wes answered.

CHAPTER 8

A Crippling Blow

AMERICAN FLAG FIRED ON!

On April 14, 1861, newspapers across the United States carried the startling news that at Fort Sumter the American flag had been fired on by other Americans. The long, bitter argument about slavery finally had boiled over. The country seethed with preparations for a war between the northern and southern states. President Lincoln sent out a call for troops to defend the Union.

91

Wes was one of the first to join the northern troops, in the Twentieth Illinois Volunteer Infantry. For the Company Descriptive Book, he offered the information that he was twenty-seven years old, and five feet six and one-half inches tall. He weighed scarcely one hundred and twenty pounds.

Because he had attended college, he soon was promoted to the rank of second lieutenant. His uniform was a dark-blue frock coat with large eagle brass buttons, a stand-up collar, and cuffs edged with light-blue braid. The regulation trousers hung over his shoetops. He wore his soft blue hat at a crooked angle.

After a short training period, the Company's commanding officer ordered, "Be ready to move to the front."

"Hooray!" the men cheered. The sooner they met the enemy, the quicker the Union forces would end the war. Or so they thought.

With his regiment, Lieutenant Powell was sent to Cape Girardeau (*jih rahr' doh*),

Missouri. This was a small Mississippi River port located on a bluff one hundred and fifty feet above the water.

During his free hours, Powell explored the countryside. This time, however, he was not interested in geology. He had studied several books on military science explaining how to build defenses to protect important military points. Since Cape Girardeau was a valuable river lookout, northern officers were sure the southerners would try to take it. So, on his own, Powell not only figured how the Cape could be defended; he also studied the countryside to learn where troop trenches could be dug, or bridges built, or enemy approaches best cut off.

His commanding officer noted Powell's interest and ordered him to design and overlook the building of works to help defend the city of Cape Girardeau. Powell's design called for four triangular forts to be built to guard the four corners of the Cape, these to be connected by high earthen walls encircling the town.

After finishing this job, Lieutenant Powell
taught a group of men how to work the
cannons. On October 8, 1861, he was made
Acting Captain of Artillery.

When Brigadier General Ulysses S. Grant
inspected Cape Girardeau in mid-November,
Powell took him on a three-hour tour. General Grant praised Powell highly for his work

and invited him to supper. Afterwards, while
they were enjoying cigars, Acting Captain
Powell dared ask a personal favor of General
Grant. "Sir, if at all possible, I would like a
week's leave of absence."

The General was surprised. "You must
have a good reason to ask for a leave at this
time, young man."

Powell's cheeks reddened. "Yes, sir, I do
have a good reason. At least, I think so. I'm
very fond of a certain young lady in Detroit.
I've kept her waiting quite a while. I — she
— we'd like to be married."

A smile lighted the General's face. He rubbed his bearded chin. "I guess the war can wait one week, Captain. Please give my best wishes to the young lady. Permission for one week's leave is granted."

Acting Captain Powell saluted smartly. "Thank you, General!" He hurried away to write to an attractive young lady named Emma Dean. For several years she and Wes had exchanged letters and visits. Wes had not proposed marriage because his river excursions had taken up his summers and all his spare money. But now that he was receiving a captain's pay, he could support a wife.

On November 28, 1861, in the First Baptist Church in Detroit, Emma Dean and John Wesley Powell were married. They returned to Cape Girardeau, the bride to a small apartment in town, the groom to his Army camp.

Although General Grant had promised immediate action, it was three more months before the troops moved to Pittsburgh Landing, Tennessee, on the west bank of the Tennessee

River. The campsite was on a tableland
dotted with meadows and oak forests. When
General Grant placed his headquarters
nearby at Savannah, Tennessee, eight miles
down the river, Emma moved there also.

The Union troops prepared for battle.
The scouts reported that the southern troops
were closing in. Wes rode out with his men.
He saw the guns rolled into place. He was
quiet and business-like. The soldiers under
him took courage from his calm.

At dawn the shooting began. Troops
poured onto the meadows and fought hand-
to-hand. But before long, it was obvious to
the northerners that they had made a costly
error. The southern soldiers greatly outnumbered them. The troops from the North
suffered many losses. The hoped-for victory
turned instead into a dreadful defeat.

Powell kept his men firing so that the foot
soldiers would have a chance to retreat.
When he raised his right arm to signal another round from the cannon, a bullet struck
his arm. Calmly, in spite of great pain,

Powell commanded his men, "Don't give an inch! Man the guns!"

General Wallace ran over to Powell. When he saw his shattered arm, Wallace said quickly, "Take my horse and ride to the hospital boat at the Landing. We're almost surrounded. There's little more you can do."

Wes was so weak that he had to be helped into the saddle. Though shock and loss of blood made him dizzy, he reached the Landing. Hours passed before the boatload of wounded men traveled downstream to Savannah. Those who were too badly injured to walk were carried to the hospital in canvas stretchers.

"Take this man to surgery immediately," a doctor said after examining Wes. "That arm will have to come off, or he will die."

Because Wes was a healthy man, he lived, though his right arm did have to be taken off. He was ill for weeks. Emma soon arrived to take care of him and others in the ward.

Other wounded men cried and raved. Captain Powell did not. He gritted his teeth.

Only Emma knew how heartbroken he was.

In time, he moved to her apartment. She tried to help him. "Don't give up any plans for the future, dear. What if you do need help with little things like tying your tie, or knotting your shoelaces? Let me be your right hand." Softly she added, "Try to be patient, Wes. Give yourself more time to get over this."

Be patient. Give yourself more time. Wes sighed. It seemed that for years he had had to do both.

How difficult it was to learn to dress himself! He hated asking for help, even from Emma. Learning to write left-handed was the worst trial of all.

Some of the soldiers in his outfit came to call. "When are you coming back to us, Captain?" they asked.

Wes paled. The Army had no use for cripples. "I'd like to, but —"

"Every able-bodied man has to do his part, sir. We've suffered heavy losses. We all have to pitch in, or we won't win this war."

99

Every able-bodied man . . . They didn't think of him as crippled? For the first time in months, his spirits lifted. "I'll be back in uniform as soon as possible," he promised.

From that time on, Captain Powell ignored the loss of his right arm. He acted as if he had never had a right arm. From June, 1862, until his release in January, 1865, he served in Tennessee, Virginia, and Louisiana. General Grant allowed Emma to travel with her husband wherever he went. As the northern victories became more numerous, Captain Powell's duties took up less of his time. He and Emma spent many happy hours gathering modern shells and fossils from Richmond, Virginia, to New Orleans.

In 1864, in Detroit, Captain Powell had a second operation on his arm. He had never been free of pain. While he was still in the hospital, he learned that he had been made a major in the Army.

"Oh, Wes, how wonderful!" Emma exclaimed. For the rest of their lives, she referred to her husband as "the Major."

After leaving the Army, the Major and Emma visited the Powell family at Wheaton.

"Now, get yourself a job teaching, and settle down," his father advised.

Settle down? John Wesley Powell knew he couldn't. He had spent too many years moving about. The childhood longing to visit new, exciting places was still strong in him. Recently he had read the reports written by General John C. Fremont about his explorations through the Rocky Mountains in the 1840's. The descriptions of the wild, high country burned in Powell's mind. He had to go west, somehow. His big problem was how to earn a living and travel too.

One of the positions offered him was professor of geology at Illinois Wesleyan University, at Bloomington. The salary was only one thousand dollars a year. But the word *geology* brought back fond memories of George Crookham, now dead, and Dr. Mather.

"But I don't know enough about the subject to teach it," he worried.

"You have months to study up on it," Emma pointed out.

The Major knew that in North America geology was still a young science. There were great stretches of mountain country west of the Mississippi that had never been seen by a geologist. And now that many people were streaming westward in search of land, there was much a geologist could do to be helpful.

Slowly an exciting idea began to take shape in Powell's mind. As far as he knew, no one had ever led a natural history excursion into the mountains. A botanist or two had gone through the Colorado mountain parks, gathering alpine flowers. But no careful, broad study of the *flora* and *fauna* had been made. So, if he taught geology during the school term, he could conduct field excursions in the summer!

"I'm going to accept that job," he told Emma.

CHAPTER 9

Only a Beginning

For the first time in his life, John Wesley Powell could call himself a scientist. His classes in geology were popular with the students. He took them on long walking trips on which they saw the geology of Illinois first-hand.

In the long winter evenings, he and Emma worked on their shell collection. Together they mounted and labeled six thousand of the shells from the Mississippi River and its streams. In the spring, the collection was shown at Illinois State Normal University.

People came from miles to view it. The long hours of work paid off handsomely. To Powell's delight, he was named director of the Illinois State History Society's museum. The directors of the Society agreed to donate five hundred dollars towards Powell's expenses if he would explore the mountain-park country of Colorado and bring back alpine plants, birds, insects, small animals, and minerals. These would make the Society's museum the best in the Midwest. Powell was to lead the first scientific natural history excursion in the western United States! He could hardly believe his good luck.

From four railroads, the Major obtained free transportation for his party and supplies. The United States War Department furnished three months' rations. The Smithsonian Institution lent him much-needed expensive instruments. Two other groups gave Powell six hundred dollars for expenses.

In early June, 1867, the thirty-three-year-old Powell hustled his party aboard a west-bound train. Emma, newly informed on wild flowers, was along. Her companion was her husband's sister, Nell. The Major had invited Nell's husband, Harry Thompson, because he was a fine map-maker. The eight others were teacher-friends, like the botanist Thomas J. Burrill, and students. All were beginners, even the Major. None had graduated from a famous university. All agreed good-naturedly that they were "shirt-tail" scientists.

At Council Bluffs, Iowa, the train crossed the Missouri River on a high bridge. On the far side the group had a glimpse of Omaha, Nebraska. They left the train a few miles farther west. They put their baggage and supplies into two wagons. Students would handle the teams. Emma and Nell settled on a wagon seat. "Colorado, here we come!" they called out gaily. Linen dusters, veiled hats, gloves, and parasols protected them from the sun and road dirt.

"Ready?" the Major asked the others. He was wearing his second-best wool suit, a blue shirt, and a string tie. His auburn sideburns already were powdered with yellow dust. Beads of perspiration ran from his hatband to his chin. He could feel the sun toasting his nose.

"Ready!" the men shouted, mounting their horses. They moved at an easy pace over the open, grassy plain.

Ten miles farther, the Major stopped on the south bank of the Platte River.

"Are we going to stop this early?" Burrill asked. The sun would not set for hours.

"You're all new at setting up camp. Let's allow plenty of time," he said, dismounting.

They would need time, because trouble began right away. The men didn't drive the stakes to which the horses were tied deep enough into the ground. The horses pulled them out and ran away. Rounding them up took several hours. Then the tent pegs weren't pounded deeply enough, and the ridge poles weren't set right, so the tents

collapsed. The students built too big a bonfire. It scorched both the cooks and the food.

To top it all, Major Powell insisted on
making biscuits.

"You've never made biscuits before!"
Emma exclaimed.

"Oh, yes, I have. There's nothing to it
when you make them Army-style."

He opened the flour sack, dumped in some
salt and soda, scooped a shallow hole and
filled it with river water. He stirred briskly
with his fist, ignoring the dust and insects
blowing onto the sticky dough. After that, he

pulled off handfuls, dropped them in a baking pan, and set the pan in a portable sheet-iron oven.

Emma and Nell struggled with smoke, spattering grease, and pots that boiled over. Finally they called, "Come and get it!"

The men grabbed their tin plates. Everyone was too hungry to complain about charred ham and scorched potatoes.

After one bite of a leaden biscuit, though, Harry Thompson said, "These are Army-style biscuits, Major?"

Powell smiled. "Yes. What do you think of them?"

Thompson shook his head. "If our soldiers ate biscuits like these, it's a wonder we won the war!"

Everybody burst out laughing, even the Major.

"Oh, the next batch will be much better," he promised.

"No!" all protested loudly, groaning and rolling their eyes.

"You stick to rocks, Major, and leave the

biscuit-making to your wife," Burrill suggested.

The Major chuckled. "All right."

The expedition traveled westward from ten to sixteen miles daily. Every member had special duties. Some collected flowers, butterflies, and insects; some dried, pressed, and identified them. Others trapped or shot small animals and birds. Other jobs were stretching the skins, cleaning skeletons, and labeling minerals, soils, and fossils. The Major rode and hiked, noting "unusual evidences of erosion" in the broad Platte Valley. Thompson worked on his maps.

Within three weeks the party experienced sunburn, sandspurs, unruly horses, burned food, mosquitoes, and drenching rainstorms. They all worked hard during daylight hours. At night, they put out the small cookfires and built one huge bonfire. Then they sang.

At night the men took turns standing guard against Indian attack, though none threatened. Whenever they rode over ruts worn nearly thirty years earlier by pioneers on the

Oregon Trail, they were reminded that this was still the frontier. Nebraska had been made a state only a few months earlier, on March 1, 1867.

Soon they had a new experience. A spicy perfume filled the air. It tingled their noses. "What is it?"

"*Artemisia* — sagebrush! This gray-green low shrub you see all around you," the Major explained. He put a sprig in his hatband, and inhaled deeply. "When you smell sagebrush, you're really out West."

The plains were vast and rolling. The land rose gradually toward the foothills of the Rocky Mountains. By the last week in June they were crossing the Bijou Basin, fifty miles east of Denver, Colorado. A fine drizzle cut off their view. About four o'clock one afternoon, the sun broke through and a double rainbow arched the sky. The clouds lifted, revealing the abrupt, massive upthrust of the Front Range.

"The Rockies!" everyone cheered. For those who had known only the grainfields and

111

sheltering wood lots of the Midwest, this was a soul-stirring sight.

A barely passable road led to the top of the Rampart Range. They gazed southward. Sprawling foothills lifted from the plain, forming giant steps to a great, snowy, cloud-crested peak.

"That's Pike's Peak!"

They oh-ed and ah-ed at the view of the famous peak and of the sun-drenched plain far below. There were pine forests on the north, and ranges of mountains, one behind the other, stretching endlessly to the west.

"Major, can't we stop long enough to do some collecting here?"

They scurried atop Rampart Range, a broad, forested mountain. There they found new birds and insects. Emma, Nell, and Burrill gathered alpine lilies, forget-me-nots, and red paintbrush. They couldn't move without stepping on flowers.

Finally the Major said, "It'll soon be sunset. We must move on." He was in a hurry to reach still higher country.

The road angled part way down the Rampart. Traveling it was dangerous. In one place, the men strained on ropes to keep the wagons from crashing down the mountainside. Soon they rolled into a meadow circled with giant ponderosa pines. An icy brooklet tumbled over rocks nearby.

"What a perfect campsite!"

"Start the fire. I'm starved!"

After supper, blankets were unrolled on the soft grass. The stars seemed close enough to be swept into a butterfly net.

After several days of hard mountain travel, they moved onto a high saddle between two peaks. This was a flower-bright meadow twenty miles long. It was ribboned with streams flowing from great snowbanks. Since no party of scientists had ever collected there, they stayed almost a month.

In the pre-dawn hours of July 27, the Major, Emma, and six others prepared to climb Pike's Peak. The men put on heavy trousers and sturdy boots. They strapped blankets behind their saddles. One student filled a back pack with cold biscuits and meat.

Emma's outfit of waterproof material came to the top of her high-buttoned shoes. She anchored her hat with a green veil, and wore black cotton gloves.

The first part of the climb was made on horseback, Emma riding sidesaddle. It was slow going. Their horses picked their way around fallen timber and jagged boulders. After twenty miles of hard riding, they reached the foot of the first ridge. Here they dismounted, and led their animals up a steep trail to the top of the ridge. They panted and tired easily at the nine-thousand-foot altitude.

During a brief stop, they collected and took notes. Then they rode along the ridge till they reached the foot of a second one. After dismounting, they topped this second ridge too.

"Phew! Let's rest and have a bite to eat!" Emma suggested.

The Major studied the peak soaring above them. This second ridge joined the main

114

mountain. He hoped they could be at the top by two o'clock.

They climbed, mostly on foot, leading their horses. On either side, the trail dropped away for thousands of feet. The dizzying heights didn't bother the Major, but the others could look only at their feet.

When they came to a huge rockslide blocking their way, Powell started across on his horse. The animal slipped and almost rolled over. Rocks skidded under their feet. Both man and horse were lucky to reach safe ground again.

"We will have to go back where we started from, and climb some other place."

Powell led them back to the first ridge, and took another trail. By two o'clock they reached timber line. Above this line no trees grew. "It's too late in the day to reach the top and go all the way back to camp. We have blankets, but not enough food to last two or three meals, unless you eat lightly. How about it?"

Everybody agreed to leave the horses at the edge of the timber line. They ate a little hardtack and beef, and then resumed climbing. They pulled themselves upward, and sometimes crawled on hands and knees. They stopped often to catch their breaths.

"Look, we've reached the snow!" Emma cried excitedly. But no one had enough energy to throw snowballs.

Shortly after that, they straightened their aching backs. They had reached the 14,110-foot-high peak.

"Hooray, we made it!" the Major shouted, tossing his hat in the air.

"Three cheers for Emma!" She was the first woman to go to the top of Pike's Peak.

116

"Hip, hip, hooray for the Major! He's part mountain goat!" a student said.

They ran around on the snow and rocks, gathering insects and lichens (*lie' kens*), flowerless plants growing on the rocks. They noted the temperature and wind speed. Only the setting sun and a rising wind forced them to leave. Soon it was dark, and cold. They inched along, holding on to one another's hands or jackets.

The descent seemed a thousand miles long, but finally trees loomed before them, and they could hear the horses nickering.

"It's starting to snow!" Emma said, her teeth chattering noisily.

They built a huge bonfire and stayed awake by toasting their faces and backs, in order not to freeze.

Yet none would have missed the climb. All agreed when the Major said, "That climb was the greatest experience I ever hope to have."

For most of them, it was. But for Major Powell, it was only a beginning.

117

CHAPTER 10

First to Top Long's Peak

After a day's rest back at camp, the Major wanted to move to South Park, west of Pike's Peak, for the remaining four weeks of collecting.

"We can't move," Burrill informed him. "Our wagons are too overloaded. We've gathered far more than we ever dreamed possible."

Powell solved the difficulty. He located a

man with a mule train to take the precious specimens they had collected to Denver. Unfortunately, in crossing a creek, one mule was drowned. Water ruined many of the flowers Burrill had pressed. The other boxes traveled safely to Denver, and by ox-drawn wagon train to the railroad at Omaha.

South Park rewarded them with many

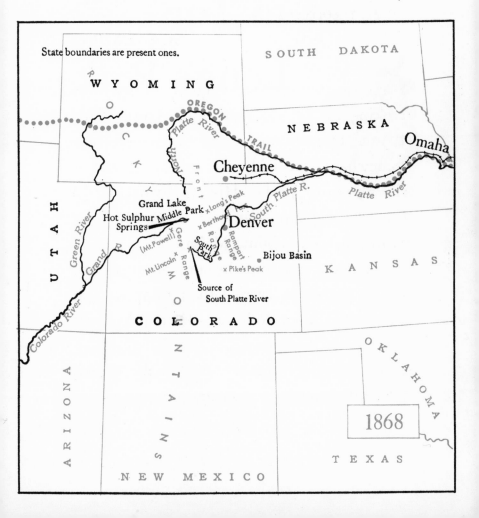

more exciting finds, including a rare squirrel. There were several hunting parties camped there. One was guided by a buckskin-clad mountain man named Jack Sumner. Since Sumner knew the mountains well, the Major questioned him about other parks and peaks. Powell thought his party was the first to examine South Park, but Sumner corrected him.

"There have been fellows in South Park before. Nope, not geologists or scientists. Surveyors for the government. They were looking for the source of the South Platte River. They didn't find it. But it's up there somewhere," he said, pointing his thumb at the glistening peaks. His eyes twinkled. "I can get away from my party for a few days. Want to scout about, Major?"

The next morning he and Sumner rode off. A packhorse carried their camping gear and food. They followed the South Platte upstream.

The river's channel narrowed. Grassy parks abounding in deer and elk and towering cedars lined the low banks. Overhead, gray-feathered camp robbers flew from tree to tree, scolding at them. Several creeks flowed into the river. Powell traced and mapped each to its beginnings. "One of these is bound to be the source of the South Platte," he said.

Creek after creek disappointed him by dividing itself into smaller creeklets.

"We must go still higher," Powell said. He led the way, floundering through soft snowbanks. He became soaked to his hips, and his feet became so cold they felt like frozen stumps. Even in the sunny, open places, he felt the icy breath of the snow-covered peaks biting through his wool clothing.

The third day they stumbled onto a grassy shelf. "Look at that swift creek! Something tells me we're on the right track at last." Excitedly Powell traced it to its source in a lake. Soaring above on his left was Mount Lincoln, on the right, Mount Triaquial. Using field glasses, Powell scanned the snowy flank between them. He spied a trickle of water falling from above.

"Come on!" He struggled upward to a tiny lake fed by melting snow from everlasting snowbanks. He stumbled around its shore. There was no inlet. He sketched the location on his field map. Then he traced a line downward, from lake to lake, to creeklet branching into creek, and finally into the river.

"This is it! We've found it!" he shouted. He had made a real discovery. He had a "first" to his credit!

On the way down, he paid more attention to the surrounding country. "Does that peak on the north have a name?" he asked his guide.

"Yes, it's Long's Peak. You know, Long was that soldier who led a military expedition out to Colorado in the 1820's. But he didn't climb the peak. Nobody has yet. I've heard tell that those who tried to have been killed."

The Major gazed long and hard at Long's Peak. His eyes gleamed as he looked at an unclimbed peak. "Maybe I'll come back next summer and tackle it," he said, half-seriously. Then he chuckled, "I'd better finish this summer's work first."

The Powell expedition remained in South Park three more weeks. A heavy snowfall and bitter cold sent them scurrying out of the mountains. At Denver, they treated themselves to hot baths, soft beds, and an elegantly served dinner at a hotel. To return to Illinois, they traveled three bone-wrenching days and nights in a stagecoach as far as Omaha, and from there on by train.

The directors of the Illinois State Natural History Museum proudly displayed the hundreds of new birds mounted, the thousands of plants and insects, the brilliant showing of minerals, and the beautiful maps that the Powell expedition brought back.

The Major asked, "Will you give money toward another expedition to Colorado?"

They agreed.

On June 29, 1868, Powell led his second party aboard a train at Chicago. He had tacked a bold banner onto the railroad car. It read "The Colorado Scientific Exploring Expedition." There were twenty-one members: the Major, Emma, Walter Powell (the Major's younger brother), a botanist named George Vasey, an artist, two newspaper correspondents, two biologists, and twelve husky college seniors. Since the Union Pacific railroad extended three hundred miles west of Omaha now, they were able to ride all the way to Cheyenne, Wyoming.

The students were surprised to see a town of four thousand people on the frontier. Many Indians were camped near the town. As soon as the party's tents were pitched near the railroad station, the Major ordered, "Divide into threes for guard duty. Each group will stand a three-hour night watch." However, they need not have worried. The Indians did not bother them.

A week passed before the Major rounded up enough saddle horses and pack mules. He did not propose to struggle with wagons in the high country. Emma was pleased when he chose a gentle, white-eyed Indian pony for her. The other horses bucked the men off repeatedly, at first. The mules gave even more trouble. But patience soon solved that.

"Does anybody know how to rope packs on a mule?" the Major asked.

No one did.

He hired an experienced packer to teach the men how to divide and pack the supplies and gear, and how to "throw" a diamond hitch. This skill could not be learned quickly. They had to adjust the loads many times on the six-day, one-hundred-and-fifty-

DIAMOND HITCH

mile journey south to Denver. Pausing only long enough to replenish their food supply, they pushed on to the west shore of Grand Lake. Their base camp was pitched at Hot Sulphur Springs.

"Howdy!" Jack Sumner greeted them all with much back slapping and hand shaking. "When do we start up the peak?"

"Not until after we get in some real work," Powell said. After all, this was a scientific expedition. He owed it to his museum directors to map and collect. Sumner didn't care. He had been hired to guide the party for the next three months.

Everyone had special duties. The Major mapped the geological structure of the mountains. He, Sumner, Vasey, and a few students roamed the Gore Range, never before explored. (Years later the highest peak in the Gore Range was named Mount Powell.)

Not until August twentieth did the Major head for Long's Peak. Six men accompanied him: his brother Walter, Sumner, three students, and Sumner's brother-in-law, William

N. Byers. A wealthy sportsman, Byers was also editor of Colorado's biggest newspaper, the *Rocky Mountain News,* published at Denver.

With one mule carrying ten days' rations, they covered four miles of a steep ridge snarled with fallen trees. The next day, they camped at timber line. With instruments, the students figured the altitude at 11,500 feet above sea level.

On August twenty-second, they started out again. Twice they came to sheer drop-offs, and had to retrace. Then they fought their way through a snowbank, only to have to turn back again.

"I think we would do better on foot," Powell decided. The horses would not wander far because of the downed timber. With back packs lightly filled with a few instruments, biscuits, and other articles, the seven men hiked up another slope. The climb made their knees shake, and their hearts pound. Several suffered nosebleeds. At one place they crawled along a knife-edged ridge with a dizzying drop on either side. On reaching the top, every man groaned. The ridge cut off abruptly in an impassable chasm.

Powell wiped his brow. "No choice, boys. Back to camp we go." He knew now why the fourteen-thousand-foot-high peak had not been successfully climbed before.

Sumner scratched his chin. "You go on back. I want to poke about. Mind if Keplinger keeps me company?" Keplinger, one of the students, was an excellent climber.

Back at camp, Powell and the others rested. Sumner returned at dusk. When Kep failed to return when darkness fell, the Major had beacon fires lighted. Not until ten o'clock did the weary student stumble in. But he had good news. He had found a way to reach the summit.

At dawn the next day, they started out across a vast, dangerous rockslide. Then they climbed till they were only seven hundred feet from the top. But a great block of sheer-walled rock stopped them.

Powell examined it closely. The rock had

cracks in it that would serve for foot- and hand-holds.

Single file they inched upward: Keplinger in the lead, then the Major, Sumner, Byers, and Walter. Farrell and Garman, the two other students, followed. Each fitted his foot in a tiny crack, dug his fingers into another crack overhead, and worked his other foot into another small hollow; found another toehold a little higher, hugged the wall, and climbed to it; and the next, and the next. This was doubly dangerous for a one-armed man, but Powell never once flinched. All clung to the wall like flies. They grunted; the thin air hurt their lungs; their hearts beat painfully. One misstep meant being dashed to death on the rocks far below.

About ten o'clock, Kep straightened up. They had nearly reached the summit. He turned to help the Major, but Powell shook his head. He meant to go the final inches on his own. Soon all were standing atop Long's Peak. The wind beat at them so hard that it was difficult to keep their balance.

129

"We made it!" they cheered, waving their hats.

They bowed their heads as Powell offered a prayer of thanks. The students built a cairn, or mound of stones. At the base they placed a can containing a piece of paper on which each man had written his name. Powell added the date, the temperature, and after it was observed, the elevation. Long's Peak proved to be 14,255 feet high. Last, Powell anchored an American flag in the cairn.

The others walked about. The top con-

sisted of a rocky area about six acres broad.
The students scraped some tiny lichens and
mosses from protected cracks in the rock.
They found only small patches of snow.

Powell looked down on Grand Lake, a
small sapphire-colored body of water glitter-
ing among emerald-green pines. He saw
Pike's Peak, Berthoud Pass, Middle Park,
and South Park. He looked beyond the Gore
Range. He checked the course of the Grand
River (now called the Upper Colorado)
from where it flowed out of Grand Lake. He
was puzzled by a dark line far, far out.

Sumner knew about that line. "The canyon of the Colorado. Indians say it's so deep,
it goes to the center of the earth." He
chuckled, then added, "The Grand flows into
it out there somewhere. No white man has
made it even halfway down the Grand."

"You're sure the Grand has never been
explored? Not mapped — I mean *explored*,"
the Major said, his interest quickening.

"Positive. No trappers, no surveyors, no
Indians, *nobody* has seen the lower canyon of

the Grand, let alone where it's supposed to join up with another big river, the Green, to form the big Colorado River."

Ideas raced through Powell's mind. As a geologist, he found the possibility of deep canyons tremendously exciting. A really deep canyon might expose the oldest rocks on the continent. So far no really old rocks had been discovered within the United States. The great Canadian geologist, Sir William Logan, had found some rocks on the Canadian shore of Lake Superior which were millions of years older than any of those ever found in the United States.

Maybe, Powell thought, in the jumbled peaks or canyons of the Colorado River or its tributaries, there might be rocks hundreds of millions of years old! For a geologist, there could be no greater achievement than locating and mapping them.

"If I come back next year, will you explore down the Grand River with me? Maybe we could find a way to explore all of it, and the Colorado too."

133

"I'll throw in with you on that! I've always wanted to see where those two rivers come together. But Major, we don't need to wait until next year to get started. Instead of going home in September, why don't you and I explore as much of the upper Grand River as we can, before snow flies? September is a good month out here."

When they returned to Grand Lake, Powell's mind was made up.

But first, he must tell the story of climbing Long's Peak to a famous newspaperman vacationing in Colorado. He was Samuel Bowles of the Springfield (Massachusetts) *Republican*. Even more than William Byers and the correspondents in Powell's party, Bowles brought nation-wide fame to Major John Wesley Powell as the conqueror of Long's Peak.

But Mr. Bowles ended his story by stating, "The great and final object of the expedition is to explore the Upper Colorado River and solve the mysteries of its three-hundred-mile canyon. . . . The maps from Washington that

134

put down only what is absolutely, scientifically known leave a great blank space here. . . . Is any other nation so ignorant of itself?"

That ignorance would be short-lived, Major Powell vowed. He aimed to tackle those blank spaces, and fill them in.

CHAPTER 11

White Water

I'll have to find another way,"
Major Powell admitted several weeks later.
He and Sumner stood on the brink of the
deep, rugged canyon of the upper Grand
River. They had fought their way through
country too broken and steep for horses or
mules. A thousand feet below them, the
river roared and tumbled over huge rocks.
"Boats could never get through there. This

136

is not the way to reach the Colorado River."

"You're not going to give up the idea of finding those old rocks, are you?"

"Definitely not. But this is as far as we dare go now. Don't worry, Jack. We aren't licked yet."

The two returned to Denver and parted company. Sumner returned to his camp in the mountains, and Powell traveled east by stagecoach and train.

While teaching in Illinois that winter, the Major studied all the maps of the region surrounding the Colorado River drainage system. He found what he thought was the best way to reach it. This was by starting from Green River Crossing, in southwestern Wyoming. The Union Pacific railroad now reached that far. Thus it would be easy to ship the tons of supplies, and the boats needed for the great adventure.

On May 24, 1869, the ten men of Major Powell's "Colorado River Exploring Expedition" embarked from Green River Crossing. Three sturdy oak-ribbed rowboats, twenty-one feet long, bobbed on the muddy Green River. It was the northernmost source of the Colorado River. The Green's headwaters rushed down from distant Fremont Peak. Specially designed by the Major, the rowboats were heavily loaded with rations and equipment. Bow and stern decks, front and back, provided storage room.

A smaller pine pilot boat was christened the *Emma Dean,* for Emma, now staying in Detroit with her family. Capable Jack Sumner would man its rear sweep. The sweep was a long, rudder-type oar locked into the sternpost. Sumner would use it to guide the boat. The oarsman, seated in the open center of the *Emma,* was a buckskin-clad trapper named Bill Dunn.

The Major assigned his brother Walter to man the sweep on the second boat, named the *Kitty Clyde's Sister.* His oarsman was George Bradley, an amateur geologist.

Bill Hawkins, a former ox driver, had signed on as cook. The camp chore boy was an eighteen-year-old wanderer named Andy

Hall. Hawkins and Hall were in charge of the third boat, named the *Maid of the Canyon*.

The men had laughingly agreed to call the fourth boat the *No Name*. Oramel Howland, a newspaper reporter turned mountain man, manned its sweep. His brother Seneca joined Frank Goodman on the oars. Goodman was an English sportsman. He had paid to join the expedition. The men would receive no pay, only plain food, generously spiced with danger.

About midday Major Powell stepped aboard his pilot boat. "Push off!" he called.

Dunn dipped the oars into the water. The spring run-off had swollen the Green. Immediately Sumner sensed the threat of the current. He clasped the sweep firmly. He knew he must keep the *Emma's* nose pointed downstream. A moment's carelessness in letting it slip broadside could be disastrous.

Moments later the *Sister, Maid,* and *No Name* were away from shore. Their crews concentrated on getting used to the waddling boats. They watched for the Major's signals. Every time he spotted rocks or floating snags, he wig-wagged a white flag.

The boats swung around a bend. Two miles farther the *Emma* jarred to a halt on a sandbar. The Major almost went head over heels into the river. Sumner kicked off his moccasins. He jumped into the icy water, and pushed the *Emma* clear. "I'll fix you some rope toe-holds tonight, Major," he shouted.

Miles below, the Major warned of more rocks. The first three boats swept by safely. Oramel waited a second too long to turn the *No Name* aside. The boat scraped against a boulder. Seneca and Goodman were tossed overboard.

"Watch what you're doing!" Goodman said bad-humoredly, after he was fished out of the water. Shivering in his sopping buckskins, Seneca joked, "Wasn't hankerin' for a bath this soon, Oramel."

Oramel apologized. After this he would turn quicker.

In the late afternoon the Major pointed toward shore. This time Hawkins failed to respond quickly enough. Although Andy flailed the oars wildly, the *Maid* streaked four hundred yards beyond where the others had beached.

"Move on down," the Major said, laughing.

On shore the Major, Bradley, Walter, and Oramel climbed the banks. They walked for several miles. They noted the temperature and altitude. They examined the soil and rocks and sketched a rough geological map of the bluffs nearby. These four men would continue this scientific work throughout much of the journey.

In camp Andy and Seneca raised the tents. Hawkins cooked his first meal. He scorched the beans, biscuits, and ham. His coffee was as strong as a mule's kick.

Everyone grabbed tin plates and gathered around the pots. They wolfed down the unappetizing food. Afterwards, they stretched out, smoking and swapping stories. Powell

141

worked late, by firelight, transferring field notes to the permanent Journal.

"May 25. We start early this morning, and run along at a good rate," he wrote of the approaching dawn. He also mentioned that Sumner shot two mountain sheep, and that the party feasted on wild mutton.

For several more days the boatmen had little trouble. The riverbanks grew steadily steeper. The countryside seemed lonelier, and was trackless.

But where were the deep canyons, the wild foaming water they had heard about? An aged Ute chief had warned Sumner, "Rocks h-e-a-p high. Water go h-oo-woogh, h-oo-woogh! Water-pony (boat) heap buck. Water catch 'em!"

"Maybe so, for an Indian dugout, but not for our boats," Sumner had said, in telling the Major.

The expedition floated out of Wyoming and into Utah. Bradley wrote in his diary that this was "the grandest scenery I have found in the mountains."

On May 27, a deep canyon walled with flaming red rocks loomed ahead. Where the walls pinched closer, the channel narrowed. Through this, the water boiled and foamed.

The men whooped. "White water, at last!" they called to each other. The swift, foam-whitened water promised a fast, dangerous ride. But the Major held them above the canyon for three days while he "geologized." He named the canyon Flaming Gorge.

On May 30, he stepped aboard the *Emma*. Sumner and Dunn took their places. None wore shoes or hats, because they were sure of a ducking, or worse. The others were told to watch the fate of the *Emma* in fast water, before following.

The swift Green River hurtled the little craft forward. It rocked and bobbed wildly. Water splashed over the men. The red walls, soaring thirteen hundred feet above, seemed to close in over them. The men were deafened momentarily by the water's roar. They skimmed along. A half-mile farther, the *Emma* leaped past the head of the rapids, where the white water ended suddenly. Beyond it was quiet water, where the surface was smooth and the current less strong.

"We made it! Hurrah!" the three cheered.

Powell wagged his flag. Like race horses breaking from a starting gate, the *Maid, Sister,* and *No Name* streaked through the gorge without upsetting.

More cheers bounced against the walls.

The next day they encountered rapids made dangerous by high rocks lying in the channel. Powell wagged them all to shore. "Here's where we get our first taste of lining, boys."

The men took an instant dislike to "lining." First they had to unload the boats. Some carried the heavy boxes down the rocky shore, past the bad water. They twisted their ankles on the uneven ground. They perspired heavily, and grumbled a lot.

Others tied one hundred and thirty-foot lines to the bow and stern of each empty boat. One man carried all the bow lines below the rough water. He wound them securely around a boulder. When he waved, the men upstream let out the stern lines, one at a time. Though the river snatched the boats roughly, the men strained back on the ropes.

The hemp burned their palms. Their arms felt as if they were being torn off. They held on grimly as long as they could, so the boats would not run wild. But finally, they had to let go. The boats leaped, skimmed rocks, and floundered. Downstream the men pulled hard on the bow lines. Soon all boats were brought safely to shore and reloaded.

"Once a day of this lining business is enough!" Hawkins exclaimed, mopping his brow. Yet from here on, the crew lined hundreds of times past raging rapids.

Powell wrote in his Journal that on June 1 they made "almost railroad speed."

The men were soaked constantly. Whenever winds howled through the canyon, they shivered. Yet the sun burned their faces and arms. The rocks ripped their shoes. The repeated wetting made the flour and bacon mold. The beans sprouted.

They had passed through one deep gorge and were coming into another dark passage — Red Canyon. Its glowering walls extended for twenty-five miles. The roar of the water was louder than the cannonading the men had heard during the War Between the States. Some stuffed rags in their ears, but it didn't help much. The boats swept on, mile after mile, day after day. Suddenly, the canyon widened. The river calmed. It was so quiet that Powell whispered, "I can hear larks singing."

After two weeks, the men were still in fine spirits. Though some hoped to find beaver or gold, they found none. They joked about the tales they had heard about there being boat-devouring whirlpools, and waterfalls larger than Niagara on this river. They bragged about their boatsmanship. They became overconfident.

On June 9, the Howlands reacted too slowly to a danger signal. The *No Name* shot over a twelve-foot waterfall and disappeared in a welter of foam. Then the boat vaulted skyward, slipped into a whirlpool, twirled wildly, spun onto a boulder, and broke in two. The Howlands and Goodman struggled in the raging water. Fortunately the current swept them into shallows. The crew dragged them out, half-drowned.

The Howlands and Goodman had lost their personal gear and guns. But the real tragedy was the loss of one-third of the total rations stored on the *No Name*.

Small wonder Major Powell pinpointed the location as Disaster Falls.

On June 11, Bradley wrote: "The river is one continuous rapid. . . . We have been working like galley slaves. . . . Where we are tonight the river roars and foams like a wild beast."

Disaster struck again on June 16. The party's campsite was on a narrow sandbar. Small cedars lined one edge, a dense mass of willows the other. Suddenly a gust of wind scattered Hawkins's campfire. In a flash, the trees burst into flames. A long tongue of fire licked the ropes holding the boats. Some of the crew raced to keep them from going adrift, while others grabbed blankets and gear. Hawkins scooped up the mess kit. He tried to jump aboard the *Maid,* and missed. He sank in deep water and had to abandon the kit in order to surface.

Though all suffered burns, they saved the boats. Afterwards Hawkins poked through the blackened wreckage. All that remained was one pan, a portable bake-oven, one kettle, one frying pan, one ladle, three tin plates, and five cups. "Well, it could have been worse," he said.

Andy chuckled. "Good thing fingers were invented before forks."

The expedition pushed on to the mouth of the Yampa, a river entering the Green from the east. Here the men repaired boats and clothing. The Major and Bradley climbed eight hundred feet up the steep canyon wall, to geologize. Then they came to a place that stopped them.

"You rest, while I scout around," the Major offered, seeing that his companion was winded. Though one-handed, Powell climbed the rocks like a mountain goat.

He located a rock where frost erosion had

worn shallow footholds upward across the face of the cliff. He inched his way outward, trying to cross it. He almost reached the top. But suddenly he could go neither forward nor back. He was rimmed! There were no footholds ahead of him. Because he was one-handed, he could not work his way backwards. He couldn't move.

"Help!" he called to Bradley.

Bradley looked up. The Major was clinging desperately with one hand. His toes barely fitted the narrow stephold. Bradley retraced a short distance and before long found a way to the top of the cliff. He dropped on his stomach. He stretched but could not reach the Major's hand. He inched forward. No luck. Now he was in danger of toppling over and crashing to the rocks far below.

"Hold on while I search for a stick!" he called to Powell.

The Major's fingers and legs were shaking. "Hurry!"

Bradley looked around. There was not

even a twig in sight. He had no belt, no
suspenders holding up his pants. Then he
had an idea. He slipped off his pants. "Oh,
pshaw!" They were torn in too many places.
Off came his long, red underdrawers. He
grabbed the waistband, and lowered the legs.

When the cloth brushed his face, Powell
took a deep breath. He hugged the rock.
Quickly he reached for the cloth. For a moment his body leaned backward.

The underwear was stretching. But it did
not tear.

Bradley pulled hard. He lifted the Major just enough so that he could grasp Powell's wrist. Moments later he pulled his leader to safety.

"Whew! That was a close one!" both agreed.

But after a rest, both continued geologizing. On the way back to camp, Bradley filled his hat with wild currants. Danger was behind them for the moment, and the thought of currant jam on biscuits was exciting.

CHAPTER 12

The Race

Against

Starvation

On June 28 the expedition reached the mouth of the Uinta (*u ihn′ tah*) River (now called the Duchesne [*doo kain′*]). "There's an Indian mission thirty miles up the Uinta. Some of us had better walk up to it, to mail letters and buy some more food. Who will go with me?" Powell asked.

"I will," Walter Powell, Andy, and Goodman volunteered. Then Hawkins decided

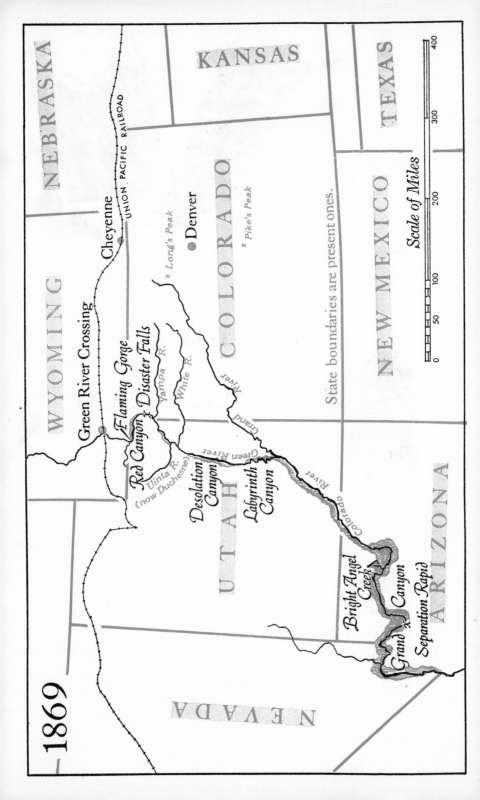

he would go, too. Those remaining would repair the boats and go hunting.

On arriving at the trading post, Goodman bade them all good-by. He had had enough excitement. Since he had shirked his chores and grumbled a lot, the men were not sorry to lose him.

Powell was disappointed on finding that the trader's shelves were almost bare. He obtained only a little flour and a few fresh vegetables. There was neither a mess kit nor other utensils. Yet all returned light-heartedly to camp, where they learned their companions had celebrated Independence Day by firing their guns and feasting on roast duck.

"All aboard," the Major called the morning of July 6. The crew rowed through quiet water past the mouth of the White River. Then they entered a region which the Major described as one "of wildest desolation." They toiled ninety-seven miles through a dangerous, gloomy, ever-deepening canyon. The Major named it Desolation Canyon.

One night they could find no sheltering brush or overhanging rocks. They had to camp on the sharp rocks. The wind blew fiercely, whipping sand over them.

Yet the Major was happy. He and his men were gathering the first scientific knowledge of this remote country. They figured the height of the canyon's walls, the speed of the river's flow, and day and night temperatures. They listed the kinds of plants, insects, birds, and animals seen. Most important, they mapped what had been unknown country.

The Major learned something else important. The river did not flow through one *continuous* canyon. A canyon could string out many miles, as Desolation Canyon did. Then suddenly the shadowy passage would widen; the steep walls would be a mile or more from the water. Instead of rocks on all sides, there would be grassy parks with trees, and birds singing, and bright sunshine. In these wider stretches, the river flowed smoothly, and so slowly that the oarsmen had to row hard.

But next, without warning, another canyon would loom ahead. The walls would hug the river. Some canyons the Major called "gorges." Gorges were the narrowest and gloomiest canyons, with the wildest water. From start to finish of this journey, he would map, and name, many canyons, gorges, and parks.

After leaving Desolation Canyon, they rowed into another canyon. Here the river turned and looped and doubled back on itself many times. Powell named it Labyrinth Canyon. On July 16, they came to a wide, deep canyon that was at right angles to that of the Green. Through its rocky channel, and from the east, flowed a great river.

"Ahoy the Grand River!" Powell and Sumner shouted. They had reached the place where two wild rivers, the Grand and the Green, joined to form the giant Colorado River.

They had accomplished one of the main goals of the expedition. They had pushed farther into the unknown wilderness than

157

any other men, white or Indian, Spanish or American. And they would map it in such detail that there would be no more mystery about this place.

"We made it!" they all exclaimed wildly as they hauled the boats up on the sandy shore. "How far is this from Green River Crossing?"

The Major answered, "Five hundred and thirty-eight miles."

Andy whistled. "It's mighty wild country. I wouldn't want to get lost in here. I'd never find my way out."

For miles and miles in every direction, there was a jumble of canyons, small and large. The rivers, the tributaries' creeks, their creeklets — all laced together in a giant-sized spider web of fearful canyons.

Though they searched, they found no sign that man had ever trod this ground before. There were no campfire ashes to be found, or arrowheads.

The crew repaired the boats again. Hawkins sifted the flour through mosquito netting

to get rid of sour lumps. He had to throw
away over two hundred pounds. He dried
the molding apples and beans in the hot sun.

As usual, the Major busied himself making field notes and geological sketches. Before leaving Green River Crossing, he had
known it was about a thousand miles from
there to the place on the Colorado where they
would leave the river. So he and his men
had reached the halfway point in their journey. Now they would tackle the second and
third goals: to map the very deepest canyons

of the Colorado, and if possible, find the oldest rocks in the United States.

"All aboard!"

On July 21, Powell led his little fleet off down the Colorado. The river was rough, with one bad rapids after another. They floated south of what is now the Utah-Arizona border. Here the rock walls were brilliantly colored: creamy orange above, then bright red, and lower, purple and chocolate brown, with green and yellow sand at the bottom. Through the shimmering heat waves, it looked like a fairyland. But it really was a grim desert.

After that, the river's course got worse. By comparison, the white water of the Green River seemed very, *very* mild. The men were tiring. Their strength was failing because of the poor and scanty food. For days they went without meat, since they could not find ducks, or deer, or even fish. Their nerves frayed from the constant roaring of the water. Daytime temperatures soared over 100 degrees.

160

About mid-August they saw a dark, narrow canyon ahead of them. Powell wigwagged everyone to shore. The sight of it alarmed the men. "Don't worry, boys. We'll get through it all right."

Bradley mopped his face. "How much farther, Major?"

"Over two hundred miles," he answered quietly.

The men gazed at the awful canyon ahead. Then they looked at each other. They weren't afraid, just tired. "We'll make it!" they said, to cheer each other.

Just before they entered what is now called the Grand Canyon of the Colorado River, or simply the Grand Canyon, Major Powell wrote in his Journal: "August 13. We are now ready to start on our way down the Great Unknown."

The walls soared three-quarters of a mile above them. Their boats tossed on the river. The sun could not reach them; the shadows were black. The gorge was so narrow that they couldn't see more than a few hundred

feet downstream. Nevertheless, they pushed
off. They rode wild waves. Water beat over
them. They had a thousand narrow misses
among the rocks sticking up in the channel.

They became so weary, and so desperate,
that they wondered how they could keep
going. Then they came to a place where a
beautiful creek trickled into the river. Here
was a sandy beach and a great willow tree.

Joyfully, Powell signaled them to shore. The
men stretched out on the soft sand. Later,
Major Powell named the clear merry stream
Bright Angel Creek.

"I hate to leave here," Andy said, sighing.

"We have to," Hawkins told him. The
food supply was down to a few pounds of
flour, a handful of dried apples, and a sack
of coffee.

Downstream, great tilted masses of black rock appeared at the water's edge. "Stop here," Powell called to Sumner. Sumner leaned on the rear sweep, and guided the pilot boat to shore.

The Major hopped out. He examined the black rocks closely. He looked for fossil shells or tiny fossil plants imbedded in them. There were none. His heart started to hammer. He must be sure. He broke up pieces of rock with his hammer.

Then he knew.

He tossed his hat in the air. "I've found them!"

At last, he had found rocks of the *Archeozoic Era,* the oldest rocks on the continent, the rocks that had existed since the beginning of the earth's history, before there was any living thing on the earth. He forgot exhaustion and hunger. He gathered samples for museums and the Smithsonian Institution. One of the greatest geological discoveries in America was his!

The crew wasn't thrilled. The men weren't

interested in old rocks. They were hungry, and this delay meant they would be hungrier.

"Major, we're running out of food," Hawkins warned his leader.

"It isn't right to keep us here," some others grumbled.

Regretfully, Powell agreed. He realized the remaining goal now was not just to complete running the Grand Canyon; it was to escape death from starvation. "All right. We'll stop all the scientific work. I'll keep making rough notes for a map, but that's all. We'll go through as fast as we can."

On August 28 they came to a place in the Grand Canyon where the danger seemed worse than ever. The half-starved crew flinched at the raging flood ahead.

"We can't run that rapids!" Bradley exclaimed. "If we do, we'll all drown."

"I refuse to run it!" Oramel Howland said. "I know I can get out of this canyon by climbing the walls and crossing the desert. At least, I have a better chance to survive going overland."

165

"I'm traveling the land route with my brother," Seneca said.

"And I'm throwing in with you," Bill Dunn added. "I've had all of this river I can take."

"What about the rest of you?" Major Powell asked.

"We're sticking with you, on the river or land."

"Please don't think we are deserting, Major," Oramel insisted.

"I know you aren't." Powell told them how much their help and companionship had meant to him — what fine, brave men they were. "You have my permission to leave." They shook hands all around. Supplied only with a few biscuits, a rifle, and bullets, the three departed.

In his Journal, Powell called this place Separation Rapid.

"To the boats!" he ordered. As always, the pilot boat was the first one to challenge the danger. It bobbed and leaped through the rapids. It passed safely, and so did the others.

On August 29 the raggle-taggle remnants of the Powell "Colorado River Exploring Expedition" emerged from the Grand Canyon of the Colorado. Beyond it, the river flowed quietly into a widening, beautiful valley. Once more the men thrilled to the sight of meadows, trees, sunshine, and birds.

"We made it! We made it!" they croaked through sun-blistered lips.

"Our work of danger was done," wrote Sumner in his diary.

The next day they met a Mormon settler, netting for fish. He prepared a feast for the bearded, starving, ragged men. They were awkward with forks.

"Butter! Cream! Meat! Real bread!"

"Melons!" Andy squealed. He buried his face in the cool, juicy sweetness.

They ate, napped, and ate again. "If only the Howlands and Bill Dunn were here," they kept saying.

An Indian carried the good news out to the nearest settlement. Another hurried word to the nearest telegraph wire. Soon all the

United States knew of the tremendous feat. Major Powell had reached and passed the junction of the Grand and the Green, where the Colorado was formed. He had found some of the oldest rocks on the continent. He had not only proved there was a mile-deep Grand Canyon of the Colorado. His party had run through it, and lived to tell the tale.

Overnight John Wesley Powell was the nation's hero.

Powell knew that from the edge of the Grand Canyon, the Colorado ran on to the Gulf of California. That part, known as the Lower Colorado, was well-known, if thinly settled. But Bill Hawkins, Andy Hall, Jack Sumner, and Bill Bradley wanted to continue down the river. As Andy said, "We've come this far. Now we're going all the way to the Gulf."

The Major was not interested in the Lower Colorado. The Army had already mapped it. He gave the crew the boats and what was left of the camping gear. He bought food for them from the Mormon. Then he waved as they pushed off. "Good-by, and God bless you all."

After they floated out of sight, he and Walter borrowed horses and rode northward. Just beyond St. George, Utah, an Indian brought bad news. The Howlands and Bill Dunn were dead. Their bodies, full of arrows, had been found by a desert water hole. Shivwit (*shihv' wiht*) Indians had killed them.

At Salt Lake City, cheering crowds greeted their arrival. After a rest, they boarded a train for the East. Everywhere people flocked to see and hear the one-armed hero. Museums and universities offered high positions to the famed explorer.

CHAPTER 13

A Harsh Place to Live

The next summer, Major Powell journeyed by train and horseback to southern Utah. Close by the small village of Kanab (*kah nab'*) he stopped at the home of Jacob Hamblin.

For a moment Powell studied this famous man. Better than any other, Hamblin knew the lonely, wind-swept plateau country neighboring the Grand Canyon. This plateau was a huge, high, almost level desert. Three bands of Paiute (*pie yute'*) Indians — the Kaibabits (*kie bah' bihts*), the Uinkarets (*oo ing' ka rehts*), and the Shivwits — had lived there long before any white men appeared. Jacob Hamblin had risked his own life to bring peace between these bands and the Mormon settlers. He was a missionary known far and wide as the Buckskin Apostle.

Major Powell introduced himself to Hamblin.

"Welcome to Kanab," the big man said, smiling. "I have heard about your trip down the Colorado."

Powell explained that he planned a second exploration of the river. His crew would be made up of all scientists. "I must have some promise from the Indians that they will not harm my men. We are not running the canyon to grab land or enrich ourselves at the Indians' expense. We won't harm them. All we want to do is carry out our scientific studies."

Hamblin understood. "Yours is a worthy

task. People need to know much more about this country. But do you mean to punish the Shivwits for killing your friends?"

"No!" the Major answered strongly. "I want only to know why they killed them, and if they will allow my second party to pass unharmed."

"Very well, I will lead you to the Shivwits. Prepare for a rough trip, Major."

On horseback, the two rode up the narrowing, cliff-rimmed Sevier (*seh veer'*) River Valley. A pack train carried their food, camping gear, a water can, and gifts for the Indians. Like Hamblin, Powell wore a fringed buckskin shirt and leggings, a soft-brimmed hat, and stout boots for tramping. During the daytime they rode in burning heat; at night they huddled against the cold around a small fire of mesquite brush. Their path lay across unmapped country. Hamblin allowed Powell time to make field notes. Several days later they came to a bubbling spring near the source of the Kanab River. Behind them towered pink, yellow, and pale orange rocks

— the Pink Cliffs. The two men made camp.

The Major noticed smoke rising miles away. "What have we there? A forest fire?"

"No, the Kaibabits are signaling. We'll have company tomorrow."

When the Kaibabits arrived, the Major's heart went out to them. They were so ragged, so thin. Small wonder! The desert was a harsh place to live.

Hamblin invited the Kaibabits to talk, for he spoke their language. He talked with the chief, and interpreted for the Major. Powell sat tailor-fashion on the ground, a notebook open on his lap. Never before had anyone, not even Hamblin, bothered to write down anything about the Kaibabits and their way of life. So far, these Indians had not been spoiled by white men.

"The chief, Chuarruumpeak (*chew ahr' rum peek*), wants a snip of your red hair for his medicine pouch. He has never seen red hair before," Hamblin told Powell.

Powell smiled, and cut off some strands of hair. "Now will the chief exchange pottery and leatherwork for tobacco, small mirrors, beads, and hand tools? Will he talk about his people?"

The Kaibabit chief was glad to talk about his people. He told the tales handed down from one chief to another: about the Great Spirit, about animals, about brave warriors. Powell wrote until his fingers could no longer hold the pencil.

After that, the Indians sang and danced for him. He described their songs and dances in his journal. The Kaibabits did all these things because they liked Powell. He was gentle. He made them feel important. They guided him to the place where the Uinkarets were hiding. This was a pine-covered butte called Uinkaret, the Place of Pines, home of the Uinkaret Indians. Here the Kaibabits turned back.

The Uinkarets were also friendly. They talked, sang, and danced for the man "who makes many scratches with a stick." They had never seen a man write before.

After receiving gifts, the young Indian men

174

staged a rabbit drive. Some spread out in a big circle. On signal, they began shouting and beating drums. The rabbits hiding under the mesquite bushes leaped away. But they all ran toward the center, into a big net,

where the women caught and killed them.

While the rabbit meat cooked, the women served Powell cactus fruit. It was sweet and almost tasteless, but it was good to a thirsty man. Then they showed him how they gathered beetles and ground them up to make meal cakes. Powell tasted one, to be polite.

The Uinkarets gave Powell an Indian name. "You, Ka-*pur*-ats," the chief said.

"What does that mean?" Powell asked Hamblin.

"It means One-Arm-Off. They trust you like a brother."

The Major was happy gathering information on these Uinkarets.

He remembered how poor and disliked the Indians in the eastern United States were; how their arts and handicrafts had almost disappeared. He remembered how George Crookham had gathered their handwork for his museum. He had promised his kindly teacher that someday he would try to help Indians. Here was his chance.

"I am not going to allow the same thing

to happen to these Kaibabits and Uinkarets, as happened to our eastern Indians. They are among the earliest settlers on the North American continent. We must preserve the story of their past and their handicrafts before their way of life is spoiled forever. I'd like to spend the rest of my life gathering information on our Indian tribes," Powell suddenly announced to Hamblin.

"Wonderful! But what about your canyon studies, Major?"

Powell had risked death to find ancient rocks. He couldn't give up geology. But neither could he turn his back on the Indians.

A few days later, Hamblin and the Major met the Shivwits at Pipe Springs, where they were hiding. They were a small people, half-starved and timid.

Hamblin told them, "Do not be afraid of my friend Kapurats. He will not harm you. Come, sit down and talk with us." When they did, Hamblin explained that Kapurats wanted only to travel the great red river in his water-pony. He was not looking for gold.

He did not want land. He wanted only to be friends. Would they let his water-pony-braves pass unharmed?

After receiving gifts, the Shivwits agreed.

Then Hamblin asked them, "Why did you kill Kapurats's friends?"

Ashamedly, they confessed. They had mistaken the Howland brothers and Bill Dunn for some other white men who had killed their wives. It would not happen to Kapurats's friends again.

After a visit with them, the Major then asked Hamblin, "Are there any pueblos near here?" By pueblos, he meant old Indian villages in which the houses were made of adobe, sun-dried bricks of clay and sand.

"Yes, if you don't mind a five-day ride across the desert."

"Mind? I should say not. When can we start?" Powell asked. Not even heat and thirst could hold him back.

On the way, he mapped more of the country and gathered plants and insects. After five days of exhausting travel, they came in sight of the old town of Oraibi (*oh rie' bih*), a Hopi (*hoh' pee*) village. It was located atop a mesa. The mesa was a great block of land that towered abruptly, with steep walls, above the surrounding desert. To reach the top, they climbed an old trail. They found that most of the Oraibis had deserted the mesa. Only a few walls of their buildings that had

been built decades ago had crumbled, however.

"Why did the Hopis build up here?" the Major wanted to know.

"They want to be safe from the war-like Navajos (*nav' ah hohs*) and Apaches (*ah patch' ees*)."

"But don't they have to haul water up here?"

"Of course."

Powell had passed the corn, squash, and melon fields planted on the desert floor by the remaining dwellers of Oraibi. Powell shook his head. How difficult life must be for the Hopis! Yet they managed to make beautiful things — pottery, weaving, masks, and colorful ceremonial costumes. He paced off the size of the town, the buildings, and the Hopis' food storage rooms, family rooms, and assembly hall. The Major wanted to be the first man to send drawings of the pueblo to the Smithsonian Institution in Washington, D.C.

For two months Major Powell studied

Oraibi and six other Hopi pueblos. That fall, 1870, he returned to Illinois to teach and organize his second expedition to the Colorado River.

In late May, 1871, the eleven men of the second party left Green River Crossing with new boats and expensive instruments. The pilot boat was christened the *Emma Dean II.* The thirty-seven-year-old Powell lashed a chair to the middle bulkhead. From this he wagged his signals.

His crew was eager to explore and study. None of the first crew was along. This time Harry Thompson was second-in-command. A photographer would take many pictures. Later, people all over the United States and the world would see what this canyon was like.

The Major should have been extremely happy. He was, for a while. Then he grew restless. The river wasn't new to him now. But there were Ute (*yute*) and Paiute tribes nearby which would be new and exciting to study.

181

He asked his map-making brother-in-law, "Thompson, if I outline the canyon studies I want made, can you carry them out? I want to leave the river and visit the Indians."

"Of course," Thompson agreed.

Powell spent months taking notes on the Utes and the Paiutes. In the midst of his tiring work, he had an idea. He knew that it would take years to gather information on the Indians of the Southwest. He also knew that it would takes years to complete a study of the Colorado River, its tributaries, and its surrounding plateaus.

"Maybe the United States Congress would help," he told himself. There was no harm in asking. Before long, Powell left the Southwest and traveled to Washington, D.C. To senators and congressmen there he presented his idea.

"The Indians all over America should be studied," he told the lawmakers. "All the studies should be centered in one government department."

The men were impressed with Powell's work, but eight years passed before they agreed to set up a department devoted to Indian studies. The department was to be called the Bureau of American Ethnology, and Powell was named director.

With his help, Congress also founded a United States Geological Survey the same year, 1879. Before long, Powell also headed the Survey. As director, he planned rock studies and mapping of the entire United States.

As no other man had done before him, he made science help his countrymen by providing them with much-needed information.

When he finished this great service, America was no longer ignorant of itself.

CHAPTER 14

The Pied Piper of Science

"I'm worn out," Major Powell admitted in 1894, when he was sixty years old.

"I shouldn't wonder," Emma said. "You've done the work of ten men. It's time you retired."

"Retired!" the Major almost exploded. He wasn't ready for a rocking chair yet. However, he had trained many fine, younger men to carry on the work of the United States Geological Survey. He could retire from the Survey. "That would leave me more time for my Indian studies," he said.

Even after resigning as director and retiring from the Survey, he worked "full time." This time he dug for Indian relics along the New England coast. For seven years, he was in much demand as a speaker. He wrote articles for scientific publications.

Summers in Washington, D.C., were hot and steamy. The man who had weathered canyons and desert heat now found his strength lessening.

Emma suggested, "Why don't we vacation in Maine? It's cool there."

Maine? An interesting coast line, geologically, thought the Major. And fascinating Indian diggings. They could keep him interested. He couldn't bear a vacation of do-nothing days. Resting was for *old* men. Maybe his legs were giving out, but his spirit and curiosity were still young. "Yes, let's go to Maine."

At Brooklin, Maine, the Powell family settled in a comfortable cottage. Pine trees filtered the sun. The front porch faced a tiny, sun-dappled harbor. Mornings, the Major rose early. He donned a knee-length wool bathing suit and old hat. He took a dip in cool water. Afterwards he dressed in knickerbockers, jacket, and boots. He walked up and down the rocky coast.

Soon he had a neighbor lad tagging along. He pointed out interesting rocks and plants. The two dug in a midden, a large mound of shells. Long years ago, Indians had eaten oysters and clams here. They had thrown the shells on a refuse heap. In the midden, the Major also found pottery and other relics. He told the lad the story of these Indians.

After the first walk with the boy, the Major returned smiling.

"You look so happy," Emma remarked. "What have you been up to?"

"Paying a debt," he said contentedly.

"Paying a debt? We don't owe anybody any money. What kind of debt?"

The Major explained. Many — oh, so many! — years ago, a kind farmer had introduced to him the world of nature. George Crookham had guided his footsteps along the road of science. Well, the United States still needed scientists. It needed them more than ever to keep up with other nations. "What Crookham did for me, I shall do for other lads. That way, I can repay Crookham. He helped me. I will help others. They will help still others. That way, America will never lack scientists."

The next day the neighbor lad asked, "Major, may these two fellows walk with us today?"

"Why, certainly."

Soon more boys joined the hike, until the Major was leading a small army. With his help, the lads became eager collectors. He hired a boat for natural history excursions along the coast. He sang; he recited poetry; he helped with many a clambake. He told the most exciting *true* stories the boys had ever heard: about the Colorado River exploration, about Indians, and rocks. Because he loved his country deeply, he passed on that feeling to these young Americans.

When the boys wanted to explore inland, the Major learned to ride a bicycle. Hat askew, gray beard flying, weathered face alight, he pedaled along with his noisy, happy crew. For seven years, the Major was a Pied Piper of Science.

In the winter of 1902, the Major spent long weeks in bed. But in May he insisted on traveling from Washington to Brooklin. "The boys expect me," he kept saying. "I don't want to disappoint them." But the Major's heart failed his spirit. On September 20, 1902, when he was sixty-eight years old, Major John Wesley Powell died quietly in his sleep.

He was buried with full military honors in Arlington National Cemetery.

Today a bronze tablet set in granite honors the memory of John Wesley Powell. It is set on the edge of the Grand Canyon of the Colorado. Thousands of sightseers visit it every year while viewing the canyon. When they look out over the tremendous, richly colored canyon, they think of the crude little rowboats and the brave, starving crew that first explored it. And they think of the one-armed scientist who helped America to know itself.

Author's Note

So often the heroes we read about were soldiers, or explorers, or scientists, or patriots. When I learned that John Wesley Powell was all of these and more, I wanted to write about him. All the events in this story are true. Young Wes really was stoned by older boys, and more than once, according to the record. This record does not name the bullies, and so I had to make up their names and what they probably said.

George Crookham did teach young Wes as I described. Try reading a few pages of Gibbons's *The Decline and Fall of the Roman Empire* and see how difficult it is. And since Powell kept no diaries of his Mississippi River trips, I had to be guided by the journal of another naturalist who ventured on the river.

During the Civil War, Powell really did have dinner with General Grant and asked the favor which the General so good-humoredly granted. I learned about Powell's injury and operation from books other men wrote about him. For the exploration of the Colorado River and the desert country, I followed Powell's own accounts closely and checked them against others written by his companions and by his two able biographers, Wallace Stegner and William Culp Darrah.

Some men tried to say Powell was scared while running the Grand Canyon. I searched for evidence of this, but never found the slightest hint, even in the writings of those who made the fearsome journey with him.

Chapter 14 is imagined, but founded on real fact. Powell delighted in taking young lads on excursions, and introducing them to the exciting world of natural history.

MARIAN T. PLACE

PIPER BOOKS